Christian Herrmann

Video-to-Video Face Recognition for Low-Quality Surveillance Data

Karlsruher Schriften zur Anthropomatik
Band 36
Herausgeber: Prof. Dr.-Ing. habil. Jürgen Beyerer

Eine Übersicht aller bisher in dieser Schriftenreihe erschienenen Bände finden Sie am Ende des Buchs.

Video-to-Video Face Recognition for Low-Quality Surveillance Data

by
Christian Herrmann

KIT Scientific Publishing

Dissertation, Karlsruher Institut für Technologie
KIT-Fakultät für Informatik

Tag der mündlichen Prüfung: 29. Januar 2018
Erster Gutachter: Prof. Dr.-Ing. habil. Jürgen Beyerer
Zweiter Gutachter: Prof. Dr.-Ing. Bernd Freisleben

Impressum

KIT Scientific Publishing

Karlsruher Institut für Technologie (KIT)
KIT Scientific Publishing
Straße am Forum 2
D-76131 Karlsruhe

KIT Scientific Publishing is a registered trademark
of Karlsruhe Institute of Technology.
Reprint using the book cover is not allowed.

www.ksp.kit.edu

Print on Demand 2018 – Gedruckt auf FSC-zertifiziertem Papier

ISSN 1863-6489
ISBN 978-3-7315-0799-4
DOI 10.5445/KSP/1000083168

Video-to-Video Face Recognition for Low-Quality Surveillance Data

zur Erlangung des akademischen Grades eines

Doktors der Ingenieurwissenschaften

von der KIT-Fakultät für Informatik
des Karlsruher Instituts für Technologie (KIT)

genehmigte

Dissertation

von

Christian Herrmann

aus München

Tag der mündlichen Prüfung:	29.01.2018
Erster Gutachter:	Prof. Dr.-Ing. Jürgen Beyerer
Zweiter Gutachter:	Prof. Dr.-Ing. Bernd Freisleben

Abstract

The increasing availability of video data is an opportunity and a challenge at the same time for law enforcement agencies. While it promises to aid in fighting crimes, manual analysis of large amounts of videos is infeasible. Automated search for persons in video data helps to answer typical investigation questions such as: Where did a suspect come from? Where did he go? Did he meet any accomplices? Face recognition methods can play a key role in answering these questions by finding occurrences of persons given query face samples. Available video data in such contexts originates mostly from surveillance cameras but might also include videos from mobile devices captured by witnesses. The resulting data quality is typically far from professional or personal footage such as TV recordings, press photographs or selfies, where automatic face recognition has already achieved impressive results, surpassing human performance in certain setups. Addressing the low-quality surveillance domain is still a significant challenge for automatic face recognition approaches, caused by reasons such as noise affection, blur, lack of effective features and low spatial resolution. In addition, the necessary large scale video analysis requires face representations to be compact to allow a fast and interactive search in the indexed video data.

The scope of this thesis is the efficient representation of detected face sequences in an index database to enable fast and accurate face search given unseen query sequences. This task includes two key parts. First, the representation of a single face image by an appropriate descriptor. And second, the fusion of a sequence of multiple face image descriptors into a single compact face sequence descriptor. Most existing face recognition approaches focus only on high-quality faces or single images. In contrast, this thesis targets low-quality video data. The lack in data quality can be counteracted by fusing temporal information across consecutive face samples in this case. Thus, the extracted face representation of a sequence is enriched by different variations of a face such as head pose, illumination or expression. Two different approaches are proposed: An unsupervised strategy, requiring no external data, and a supervised strategy leveraging public large-scale face datasets as training data to learn a robust face descriptor.

For the unsupervised strategy a multi-scale fusion concept is proposed to counteract low-resolution data sparsity for the Local Binary Patterns (LBP) face descriptor which is then combined with a face search strategy based on bag-of-words and inverted indices. This previously unsuccessful strategy for face recognition is made possible by locally built indices leveraging fixed positions of facial features such as the eyes or nose. The supervised strategy employs a specifically designed low-resolution Convolutional Neural Network (CNN) which extracts compact and discriminative face descriptors out of single face images. It is trained with a novel dataset augmentation strategy adjusting the data quality of training images to the low-quality target domain, to increase the robustness and cross-domain generalization of the CNN-based descriptors and a max-margin based loss function enabling fast training of the network and compact face descriptors which can be efficiently compared by Euclidean distance. Combined with a center-based face sequence descriptor which is motivated by the enforced compactness of the proposed loss function, this strategy allows efficient face indexing and search independent of sequence length. The evaluation is performed on surveillance-like public video datasets as well as on self-collected actual surveillance video footage. Significant improvement over state-of-the-art methods is achieved.

Zusammenfassung

Die zunehmende Verfügbarkeit von Videomaterial ist sowohl eine Chance, als auch eine Herausforderung für die Strafverfolgung. Obwohl das Material im Fall von schweren Straftaten zur Aufklärung beitragen kann, erfordert die manuelle Auswertung einen erheblichen Aufwand und stößt rasch an ihre Grenzen. Eine automatisierte strukturierte Aufbereitung mit der Extraktion relevanter Inhalte erleichtert eine Auswertung solch großer Datenmengen. Die Auswertung der Videodaten hilft dabei typische Fragen zu beantworten. Für den Fall von Tatortvideos könnten das etwa sein: Wo kam der Tatverdächtige her? Wo ging er hin? Hatte er Kontakt mit Komplizen? Verfahren zur Gesichtswiedererkennung spielen eine Schlüsselrolle in der raschen Beantwortung dieser Fragen, indem weitere Vorkommnisse einer Person anhand eines Anfragegesichts gefunden werden. Die zu durchsuchenden Videos können dabei nicht nur von Überwachungskameras stammen, sondern auch von Zeugen an Ermittlungsbehörden übergeben worden sein (Handyvideos). Die Datenqualität entspricht typischerweise nicht den Standards professioneller oder gezielter privater Aufnahmen, wie beispielsweise in Fernsehaufnahmen, Pressefotos oder Selfies. In solchen Fällen erreichen existierende Verfahren zur Gesichtswiedererkennung bereits beeindruckende Ergebnisse, welche in bestimmten Fällen sogar die menschliche Wiedererkennungsleistung übertreffen. In Videos aus dem Überwachungskontext stellt Gesichtswiedererkennung hingegen noch immer eine erhebliche Herausforderung dar. Dies liegt insbesondere an meist verrauschten Daten, Unschärfe, ineffektiven Merkmalen und geringer örtlicher Auflösung. Darüber hinaus erfordert die Analyse großer Videomengen eine kompakte Gesichtsrepräsentation, um schnell und interaktiv im indexierten Videomaterial suchen zu können.

Diese Arbeit umfasst die effiziente Repräsentation von in Videos detektierten Gesichtssequenzen in einem Index, um darin mit unbekannten Anfragesequenzen schnell und zielgerichtet nach Gesichtern zu suchen. Dazu ist zunächst eine Repräsentation einzelner Gesichtsbilder durch einen geeigneten Deskriptor und weiterhin die Fusion einer Sequenz dieser Einzelbilddeskriptoren zu einem kompakten Gesichtssequenzdeskriptor erforderlich. Die meisten existierenden Gesichtswiedererkennungsverfahren adressieren entweder hochqualitative Gesichter oder Einzelbilder. Demgegenüber zielt diese Arbeit auf niedrigqualitative Videodaten. Der mangelnden Datenqualität kann in diesem Fall durch die zeitliche Fusion aufeinanderfolgender Gesichtsbilder begegnet werden. Die extrahierte Gesichtsrepräsentation enthält dadurch verschiedene Ausprägungen eines Gesichts wie beispielsweise verschiedene Kopfposen, Lichtverhältnisse oder Gesichtsausdrücke. Zwei Ansätze werden in dieser Arbeit erarbeitet: Eine unüberwachte Strategie, die keine externen Daten erfordert, und eine überwachte Strategie, die große öffentliche Gesichtsdatensätze als Lerndaten nutzt, um einen verbesserten Gesichtsdeskriptor zu trainieren.

Die unüberwachte Strategie basiert auf einem neuen Multiskalen-Fusionskonzept für *Local Binary Patterns* (LBP), das den spärlichen Daten in niedrig aufgelöstem Bildmaterial entgegenwirkt, und einem erweiterten *bag-of-words* Suchverfahren, basierend auf inversen Indizes. Der zuvor für die Gesichtswiedererkennung wenig erfolgreiche *bag-of-words* Ansatz wird durch lokale Indizes, welche die ortsfesten Positionen von Gesichtsmerkmalen wie den Augen oder der Nase ausnutzen, ermöglicht. Die überwachte Strategie benutzt ein speziell für niedrige Auflösungen entworfenes faltendes künstliches neuronales Netz (CNN), welches die Extraktion kompakter und diskriminativer Gesichtsdeskriptoren aus Einzelbildern ermöglicht. Es wird mit einer neuartigen Datenerweiterungsmethode trainiert, welche die Qualität der Lerndaten an die Zieldomäne anpasst, um die Robustheit des Deskriptors gegenüber niedrigqualitativen Daten zu erhöhen. Eine *max-margin* basierte Zielfunktion ermöglicht ein schnelles Training des Netztes sowie kompakte Gesichtsdeskriptoren, die mittels euklidischer Distanz verglichen werden können. Zusammen mit einem mittelwertsbasierten Sequenzdeskriptor, motiviert durch die erzwungene Kompaktheit der vorgeschlagenen Zielfunktion, erlaubt diese Strategie eine effiziente Gesichtsindizierung und -suche. Die Auswertung der vorgestellten Strategien erfolgt sowohl auf überwachungsartigen öffentlichen Datensätzen, als auch auf selbst gesammeltem tatsächlichen Überwachungsmaterial. Die entwickelten Verfahren führen zu einer signifikanten Verbesserung gegenüber dem aktuellen Stand der Forschung.

Contents

1 Introduction

1.1 Motivation

The number of recorded surveillance footage is vastly increasing with the amount of installed surveillance cameras. Studies suggest 4 to 5 million installed cameras [McC03] in the UK alone. Thus, when a crime is committed, there is nowadays a high chance of available video footage of the crime scene and surrounding area which is even increased by the ubiquity of mobile devices leading to witnesses being able to record critical situations.

Analyzing these surveillance videos supports the investigation and aids crime fighting. Currently, the analysis is a mostly manual task where operators watch the recorded video to extract any desired information. Depending on the scenario, the range of potentially interesting events varies and can include extraction of hints about suspects for identification, abnormal behavior detection and inspection to identify crimes in the footage. Typical analysis questions are

- When exactly did a crime happen?
- How did a suspect arrive at or leave the crime scene?
- Where in the footage does a suspect appear?
- Did a suspect meet any accomplices?
- Who is visiting a specific place?
- Where did a specific object or vehicle appear?

Figure 1.1: Typical surveillance footage.

A repeating pattern is the search for persons. Face recognition methods can play a key role in answering some of these questions by finding further occurrences of persons given query face samples. Besides soft-biometric features (e.g., height, weight, gender, clothing, hair color) [Rei13] and gait [Tis09], the human face is the most discriminative biometric feature easily observable at a distance in video footage. Using the face for searching persons in video data has several advantages:

- Highly discriminative. Humans use faces to identify other people.
- Constant over longer periods compared to clothing.
- Difficult to alter in the sense of pretending to be someone else.
- Significant permanent changes, such as plastic surgery, are rare and usually costly.

On the other hand, relying on the face involves also some disadvantages:

- It is easy to cover partially or fully by hair, beards or accessories such as scarfs, baseball caps or masks.
- Invisible from some perspectives, especially from behind.
- Small size thus sometimes captured with insufficient quality.

To benefit from the significant advantages, this work focuses on automatic face recognition strategies suitable for surveillance video data. Available video data in such contexts originates mostly from fixed surveillance cameras but might nowadays also include videos from mobile devices captured by witnesses. Typical examples are illustrated in figure 1.1. In all cases, the data quality is usually far from professional or personal footage such as TV or press photographs, selfies or profile photos, where automatic face recognition has already achieved impressive results, surpassing even human performance in certain setups [Kum09, BR14, Tai14, Lu15, Sch15b, Bla16, Lu17]. Strategies to create a robust face recognition system under the challenginglow-quality conditions are proposed and analyzed, especially, regarding the constraint of being suitable for large scale video analysis.

1.2 Challenges

Face recognition in surveillance video data is a challenging task. The main reasons for this are poor cameras, limited storage and transmission capacities, the unrestricted capturing conditions and practical requirements. In detail, the challenges are depicted in figure 4.8 and can be categorized as follows [Her15e].

1. **Low video quality** caused by the video capturing devices and the unrestricted scenario.
   - **Low resolution** resulting in faces being only a few pixels wide originates from either low-cost cameras with a low resolution, large capturing distances or both. The typical face width is well below 40 pixels.
   - **Lens distortions** originating from low-cost camera optics. This occurs mostly for wide angle lenses and yields unnatural face proportions.
   - **Image noise** is caused by the physics of the camera sensor and its liability to quantum and measurement noise. It can obstruct at least smaller facial details.
   - **Blur** in the shape of either motion or out-of-focus blur degrades signal quality by removing high-frequency information. Motion blur results from integration over time in the image capturing process when either recording moving objects or recording with a moving camera. In particular, dark and indoor environments requiring long exposure times lead to motion blur. The degrading impact on face recognition depends on the angle and length of the relative motion [Raj14]. Out-of-focus blur is isotropic and originates often from fixed focal length optics in the camera resulting in a limited depth of field. Objects outside the designated distance range are consequently blurred.
   - **Compression artifacts** from algorithms such as JPEG or h264 degrade image quality by removing information that is potentially unimportant for the human perception. Due to limited transmission and storage capacities in surveillance installations and around-

the-clock recording, strong compression is usually applied in fixed installations to handle the large amount of data.

- **Low frame rates** reduce temporal information. Less samples and views of a face can be considered to build a face model. The reason for reduced frame rates are the same as for using compression: limited transmission and storage capacities.
- **Interlaced video** is mostly generated by older video cameras. This reduction of the vertical resolution by half in favor of doubling the temporal resolution creates artifacts when reconstructing the full resolution, especially when improperly paired with an unsuitable compression algorithm.
- **Bad illumination** leads to several challenges. Low illumination at night or indoors requires either longer exposure times leading to motion blur, or leads to increased image noise. Too strong illumination such as direct sunlight can cause cast shadows in the face or saturation of the image pixel intensities because of the limited dynamic range of the camera.
- **Unrestricted head poses** render the face matching more challenging than frontal face recognition [Fis12]. Matching faces across poses is challenging because only a minor part of the face might be visible at the same time.
- **Partial occlusion** of the face reduces the amount of observable facial features. Either face modifications, such as makeup or hair, or objects, such as sunglasses, caps or scarfs, can result in significant face occlusions.

2. **Applicability** in terms of user benefit.
   - **Generality** of methods is required to match faces from different video sources. Video quality is not only low but can also differ in every aspect between domains across which faces should be compared. Consequently, face matching strategies have to be robust against this domain shift and bridge the domain gap for robust cross quality matching.
   - **Processing large-scale video data** requires a sufficient processing speed. Efficient solutions are necessary, both in terms of indexing, i.e., collecting and representing all faces from the video footage, as well as querying with new face samples.

Figure 1.2: Illustration of typical low-quality data challenges. First row: low resolution, distortion, low illumination + noise and motion blur. Second Row: Out-of-focus blur, compression artifacts, interlacing artifacts and saturation + cast shadows. Third row: non-frontal head pose, occlusion by a cup, sunglasses and a hoodie.

1.3 Contributions

The contributions of this thesis focus on building an efficient representation of detected face sequences to enable fast and accurate face recognition given unseen query sequences. Two different approaches are explored: An unsupervised strategy, requiring no labels and no external data, and a supervised strategy leveraging public large-scale face datasets as training data to learn an improved face descriptor. The evaluation is performed on surveillance-like public video datasets as well as on self-collected actual surveillance video footage. Significant improvement over state-of-the-art methods is reported. In detail, the contributions are:

1. A completely unsupervised video face recognition chain including
    - an improvement of single image face descriptors by a multi-scale fusion concept to counteract low-resolution data sparsity for the

Local Binary Patterns (LBP) face descriptor [Her13a] and a novel feature augmentation strategy using head pose meta-data for improved cross-pose recognition [Her15a] and

- a novel face recognition strategy based on bag-of-words and inverted indices for fast matching of local features [Her15b]. This previously unsuccessful strategy for face recognition is enabled by locally built indices to leverage fixed positions of facial features, such as the eyes or nose, and by temporal fusion of local features across consecutive face samples to enrich the face model with different variations such as head pose, illumination, or expression.

2. A supervised face recognition chain consisting of
   - a new specifically designed low-resolution Convolutional Neural Network (CNN) which extracts compact and discriminative face descriptors out of single face images [Her16c, Her17],
   - a novel training dataset augmentation strategy adjusting the data quality of training images to the surveillance domain, based on a systematic analysis of the surveillance domain's image quality effects [Her15e], to increase the low-quality robustness of the CNN-based descriptors [Her16b],
   - a max-margin based loss function, which is novel in the context of CNNs, enabling a compact face descriptor which can be efficiently compared by Euclidean distance [Her16c], and allowing an effortless combination of multiple training datasets to increase the generalization power and
   - a center-based face sequence descriptor which is theoretically motivated by the enforced compactness of the proposed loss function to maximize the inter-class distance. The resulting and only 128 dimensional sequence descriptor allows efficient face indexing and search because Euclidean distance is applicable for comparison.
3. Collection of two novel video face datasets:
   - A face dataset based on large-scale TV recordings to train the supervised CNN-based face image descriptor [Her15a, Her16c].
   - The main evaluation dataset to explore low-quality video face recognition strategies on in-the-wild data has been collected from low-quality surveillance footage [Her16b].

2 Related Work

Face recognition or sometimes also called face matching is the task of comparing faces with respect to person identity. Besides iris, gait and fingerprint recognition, it is the fourth common biometric recognition task [Tis09]. The same three basic tasks occuring for general biometric systems [Li09] apply also in the special case of face recognition [Li11c, Zha11, Sha10]:

- **Face verification** means the one-to-one comparison of two face samples and to decide if they originate from the same identity. To solve the task, a similarity score between both samples is determined and thresholded to derive the final decision. Typical applications are access controls, such as border crossings, where a person's face is compared with the passport picture.
- **Face identification** assigns a previously known identity to a query sample. This involves a one-to-many comparison of the sample to a gallery of predefined faces. Closed-world identification has only to decide which gallery identity matches the query best. It is assumed that no out-of-gallery identity is presented as query sample. If out-of-gallery identities are possible, the open-world identification scenario applies and the additional decision if the query sample is included in the gallery at all is required. In either case, an alarm can be raised if a specific gallery match is observed.

- **Face retrieval** tries to find all matching face samples in an unstructured database. It provides a similar workflow as known from internet search engines. Given a query face, the result is a ranking of all faces in the database according to similarity with the query.

Face verification can be understood as the base task in the sense that a face verification system can easily be modified to be applicable for both other tasks. For face identification, the face verification scores between query and gallery samples can be compared and thresholded to solve the task. Face retrieval can be addressed by sorting the scores between the query and all database samples. In particular, the recognition performance between verification and identification scenarios is directly related under the closed world assumption [Bol05]. This means that an evaluation of the identification scenario under these conditions will provide no further information if a verification evaluation is already available. This explains the special role of face verification and its wide application for challenges and comparison of state-of-the-art results [Hua07, Wol11, KS16]. However, the relation between verification and identification or retrieval is asymmetric. This means, there exist identification [Din15] and retrieval approaches [Siv03] which are unsuitable for verification.

The final goal of this thesis is a face retrieval system which searches for the occurrences of a query face in a dataset of surveillance videos. In order to create better comparability to existing approaches, the face verification setup is addressed as well.

2.1 Face Recognition

Computer-based face recognition was first performed by [Kan77]. Using manually extracted facial feature distances from images, recognition is automatically performed based on these distances. The Eigenfaces approach [Tur91] can be seen as beginning of actual image-based automatic face recognition. It performs a Principal Component Analysis (PCA) on the vectorized image data, removes dimensions with low energy and keeps the remaining ones as descriptor for a specific face.

Nowadays, automatic face recognition has developed into a wide field due to the amount of potential application domains and arising challenges. Besides broad surveys trying to cover most general applications [Li11c, Jaf09, Zha03b, Che95] a lot of specific ones exist, covering the variety of aspects such as adverse conditions [DM14], illumination [Zou07b], pose

[Zha09, Osc14, Din16a], low resolution [Wan14b], single images [Tan06], video [Bar12], 3D [Zho14], heterogeneous conditions [Ouy16] and near infrared images [Far16].

Face recognition is a highly competitive research field and offers a lot of comparison opportunities between approaches for different domains based on a significant number of public datasets (refer to section 2.1.5) as well as organized competitions [Phi03, Phi05, Bev13, KS16].

The following sections review specific relevant aspects of image-based face recognition for this thesis.

2.1.1 Single Image Representation

Face recognition for video data can be split into the two steps of face image representation (reviewed here) and temporal sequence representation (next section).

The first popular face image recognition techniques, such as Eigenfaces [Tur91] or Fisherfaces [Bel97], are holistic representations of the face. In this case, a face is represented in a descriptor where single dimensions are unrelated to spatial features of the face, i.e., no location or region alone is completely responsible for a descriptor dimension. The simplest holistic face representation is the vectorized face image itself. It suffers from several disadvantages such as significant illumination variance and a rather high dimension for high-resolution (HR) face images.

Over time, the holistic methods were superseded by descriptors based on local features such as Gabor features [Zou07a], LBP [Aho06], Modified Census Transform (MCT) [Fro04], Local Directional Patterns (LDP) [Jab10], Local Ternary Patterns (LTP) [Lia10], or dense Scale-Invariant Feature Transform (SIFT) [Sim13, Par14]. For building these descriptors, the face image is divided into local regions and the respective feature is computed for this region only. Fusion of all local region features, usually by concatenation, results in the face image descriptor. The local regions may overlap, can be weighted differently and may also be extracted at different scales [Li14b]. When collecting local features to describe an object, it is useful to augment each local feature by its image coordinates [Li13, Par14, Sim13], which means the concatenation of the local feature vector and the normalized image coordinates of its location. They significantly outperform the older holistic descriptors for face sizes of about 64×64 pixels and above [Hei03, Aho06, Che11b]. Reasons include the preservation of spatial information by patch-wise feature application and the better illumination invariance of the features. LBPs are, for example, invariant to monotonic illumination changes because only binary information (larger/not larger) is extracted from comparison of pixel values. With decreasing resolution, less local information is available leading to a descreasing performance [Cev10].

With the increasing availability of larger face datasets, methods evolved where descriptors based on the local features are trained. Either cumulative descriptors [Li13, Sim13] or votes of trained face recognition classifiers [Ber12, Wol11, Wol13] are employed as descriptors instead of the classifier input itself. For example, the Tom-vs-Pete approach [Ber12] selected 5,000 classifiers where each is trained to discriminate between only two identities. The face image descriptor consists of the concatenated scores of all these classifiers.

Recently, previous face image descriptors are outperformed by deep CNNs (see section 2.3) trained on very large-scale datasets, which are proven to be very effective and generalizable for HR single image face recognition [Sch15b, Tai14, Par15, Sun15, Che16, Din16b, Liu16, Mas16, Ran16, Wen16, Bod17]. Strictly speaking, these CNN-based face descriptors are holistic. Although the network architecture works locally in early layers, the local information is fused at the end of the network into a holistic face descriptor. As such, it can be seen as a simultaneous learning of discriminative local features and a feature fusion strategy. When having a look at these state-of-the-art solutions, the network architecture is usually inspired [Sch15b] by or directly derived [Par15] from a network architecture designed for the ImageNet challenge [Den09]. There, images have to be classified into one of 1000 diverse categories according to the depicted object in the image. Consequently, to apply the same networks, the face image is required to have the same or a similar resolution as the ImageNet data, which is in most cases scaled to 224×224 or 256×256 pixels. Image data from personal snapshots or professional footage usually includes at least this face size, making it a feasible strategy. In contrast, video data and surveillance footage in particular lacks in resolution and requires upscaling to serve as input of such a network. Thus, some of the finer details such a network might be focusing on for the recognition are unavailable. Addressing the low-resolution (LR) challenges has received little attention early on when designing and training a CNN. The results are mediocre for the few exceptions [Law97, Duf08, Wan16]. In particular, Schroff et al. [Sch15b] reported a drop from 86.4% to 37.8% in validation rate when the face size was reduced from 256 × 256 pixels to 40 × 40 pixels. Nevertheless, recently, the combination of a super resolution upscaling network and a large HR face recognition network achieved promising results for LR face recognition [Wu16].

Table 2.1: Selected single image face descriptors.

image descriptor	holistic	supervised	dimensions
image vector	×		many
Eigenfaces [Tur91]	×	×	few
Fisherfaces [Bel97]	×	×	few
Gabor [Zou07a]			many
LBP [Aho06]			mid
MCT [Fro04]			mid
LDP [Jab10]			mid
LTP [Lia10]			mid
dense SIFT [Sim13, Par14]			many
Tom-vs-Pete [Ber12]	×	×	mid
MBGS [Wol11, Wol13]	×	×	many
DeepFace [Tai14]	×	×	mid
FaceNet [Sch15b]	×	×	few
VGG-Face [Par15]	×	×	mid

A comprehensive overview of face image descriptors is listed in table 2.1. Besides the holistic or local character, the biggest aspect is whether the descriptor is completely handcrafted (unsupervised) or requires training data (supervised). Supervised descriptors include the pitfall of overfitting, especially, if insufficient amounts of training data are available.

2.1.2 Sequence Representation

Modeling a sequence of face image descriptors allows the step from still image face recognition to video face recognition. Face sequences or face tracks are consecutive image samples of one face which are generated by a face tracker [Sha10, Li11c, Sme14]. The different sequence representation methods can be separated into the categories *set-based, mean-based, space-based, manifold-based, probabilistic* and *cumulative*.

Table 2.2: Selected face sequence descriptors overview. d denotes the image descriptor dimension and n the number of images per sequence. The numbers of checkmarks for practical compactness and speed indicate qualitatively the size of the constants which are ignored by the Big O notation. Thus, choices with better Big O complexity might turn out worse (less checkmarks) in practical applications.

sequence descriptor	**independent of length**	**compact in practice**	**fast in practice**	**space complexity**	**construction complexity**	**comparison complexity**
best-shot [Wol11]	✓	✓✓	✓✓	$\mathcal{O}(d)$	$\mathcal{O}(n)$	$\mathcal{O}(d)$
nearest neighbor [Wol11]				$\mathcal{O}(dn)$	$\mathcal{O}(1)$	$\mathcal{O}(dn^2)$
image/descriptor-level mean [Jen08, Ort13]	✓	✓	✓✓	$\mathcal{O}(d)$	$\mathcal{O}(dn)$	$\mathcal{O}(d)$
desicion-level mean [Tap12, Wol11]				$\mathcal{O}(dn)$	$\mathcal{O}(1)$	$\mathcal{O}(dn)$
MSM [Fuk05]	✓	✓	✓	$\mathcal{O}(d)$	$\mathcal{O}(dn^2+d^2)$	$\mathcal{O}(d)$
LLE [Had09c]				$\mathcal{O}(dn)$	$\mathcal{O}(dn)$	$\mathcal{O}(dn)$
Isomap [Yan02]	✓	✓	✓	$\mathcal{O}(n)$	$\mathcal{O}(dn^2+n^3)$	$\mathcal{O}(n)$
prob. distribution [Zho06]				$\mathcal{O}(d^2)$	$\mathcal{O}(d^2n)$	$\mathcal{O}(d^3)$
APEM [Li13]	✓			$\mathcal{O}(d)$	$\mathcal{O}(dn)$	$\mathcal{O}(d)$
Fisher vector [Par14]	✓	✓✓	✓✓	$\mathcal{O}(1)$	$\mathcal{O}(dn)$	$\mathcal{O}(1)$

- **Set-based** strategies model the face image descriptors of one sequence as set and select single (best-shot [Wol11]), random [Tai14], specific [Zha08a, Sch15b] or all [Che11b] elements of the set for a pair-wise comparison. Based on the pair-wise distances, popular choices for the set distance are the minimum or the Hausdorff distance [Che11b].
- **Mean-based** methods combine the face sequence into a single representation by averaging. Afterwards, the task can be treated as if it were single image face recognition. Averaging can be done over all or a selection of frames on image [Jen08], descriptor [Hu14, Ort13, Par15] or decision level [Tap12, Wol11, Wol13]. A possibility to formalize and extend this strategy are pooled kernels [Bäu14].
- **Space-based** methods model the face image descriptor space of one sequence by a linear model. Widespread options are the convex hull [Cev10] or an affine subspace in the MSM [Yam98, Fuk05]. Comparison is performed by the principle angle between the subspaces [Fuk05] or the Euclidean distance between the hulls [Cev10].
- **Manifold-based** methods choose a more complex non-linear manifold instead of a linear model for descriptor space representation. Manifold-based methods operate directly on raw pixel values because it is known that the manifold assumption holds in this case [Had04]. Many non-linear possibilities to model the face sequence are proposed, ranging from linear approximation by piecewise linear subspaces [Lee03, Lee05, Wan08] over applying LLE [Had09c], Isomap [Yan02], kernel based methods [Cev10, Sha11] or combining LLE and k-means [Had04] to local probabilistic models [Ara06b, Ara09b, Wib13].
- **Probabilistic** handling of sequences is either performed distribution-based or test-based. In the first case, the distribution of the descriptors is determined and the sequence similarity is rated by standard distribution distances [Zho06]. The second possibility consists of drawing samples from a sequence to test the identity hypothesis [Din15] with respect to another sequence.
- **Cumulative** descriptors are an elegant way to collect local features spatially and temporally with the same mechanism. For this strategy to work well, local features are usually augmented, i.e., concatenated, by their respective spatial image coordinates. Adding temporal information in shape of sequential data creates no additional burden. As

cumulative descriptors, Gaussian Mixture Model (GMM)-based descriptors [Li13] and Fisher vectors [Par14] are applied. Because large amounts of features are required to build the dense models, these methods are incompatible with holistic face image descriptors.

Besides differences in recognition performance, the key differences between sequence representations are the computational burden for calculating and comparing the sequence models, the size of the sequence model and their independence of the sequence length. Assuming a sequence length of n, an image descriptor dimension of d and one-to-one sequence comparison, table 2.2 denotes the respective representation and comparison complexity.

2.1.3 Data Quality

Similar to human face recognition performance [Bur99], automatic face recognition performance depends significantly on the data quality. The effect of data quality can best be seen for two very popular face recognition benchmarks: Labeled Faces in the Wild (LFW) [Hua07] and YouTube Faces Database (YTF) [Wol11] with example images depicted in figure 2.1. LFW is a rather high quality image dataset with a top verification performance of 0.998 at the time of writing [1]. The video data of YTF has lower quality with respect to resolution, blur and compression leading to a lower accuracy of 0.973 [Par15]. Human face recognition performance on these well studied datasets shows the same effect with 0.983 (LFW) and 0.897 (YTF) accuracy, respectively [BR14]. It can also be noted that humans have been outperformed by the automated face recognition systems in these settings [Lu15, Sch15b].

Low Resolution

Nevertheless, with face image sizes beyond 100×100 pixels and professionally produced imagery, both datasets can still be called high-quality datasets when compared with typical in-the-wild surveillance footage. There is no strictly defined limit regarding resolution where faces are considered low-resolution (LR). Once again, human capabilities serve as a first hint: For familiar faces, recognition performance is reported to saturate above 19×27 pixels face size, being still fine for 16×16 pixels and working to some extent for merely 7×10 pixels [Sin06]. This range correlates with findings

[1] http://vis-www.cs.umass.edu/lfw/results.html

about face resolutions found in computer vision literature. Depending on the face recognition method, the face size threshold where performance saturation is observed ranges from 16×21 to 48×64 pixels [Wan14b].

Figure 2.1: Qualitative comparison of face images from LFW (top) and YTF (bottom).

The common solutions to address LR data are super-resolution methods where LR images are upsampled to apply a conventional high-quality face-matching strategy afterwards [Wan05, HY08, Wan14a, Nas14] which proves to be a solid strategy for comparing LR samples to high-resolution (HR) gallery faces [Wan14b] but appears infeasible for video-to-video matching due to its processing complexity.

Another popular option to address the aspect of the low pixel numbers is to avoid explicit features at all, meaning to work with the raw pixel values as model input. This has the advantage that manifold assumptions hold which offer an elegant way to model the face space [Lee03, Lee05, Wan08].

Low Quality

In practice, low resolution alone is a rare issue because further quality degrading effects, such as blur, occur at the same time. But lack of resolution amplifies these effects unfavorably, as illustrated in figure 2.2. One option to compare low-quality faces is to mitigate the low data quality by preprocessing steps. Certain effects, such as compression [Lai02] or motion blur [Sha08], can be reverted to some extent before applying face recognition techniques. Further approaches perform direct low-quality matching, for example, via blur resistant features [Oja08]. In particular, recent low-quality face recognition strategies are still largely based on conventional non-CNN strategies consisting of a combination of local features and learned representations such as metric learning [Mud16], dictionary learning [She14, Mud17] or manifold learning [Jia16].

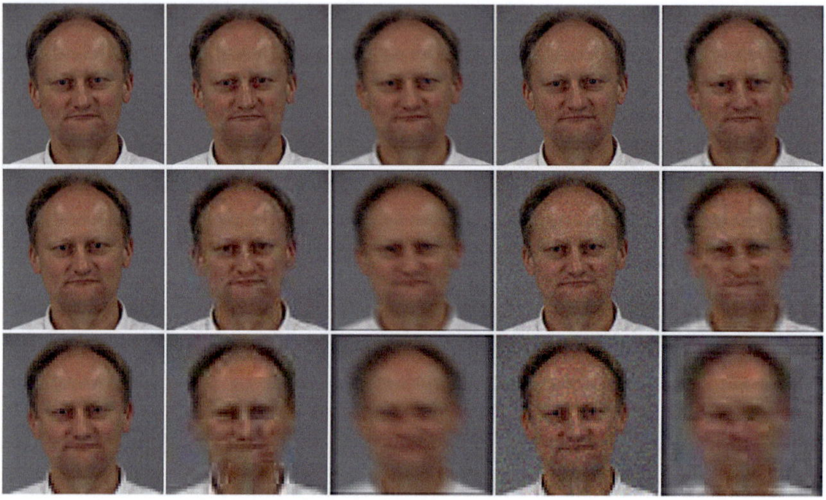

Figure 2.2: Illustration of the amplification effect of low resolution on further effects. From left to right: none, compression artifacts, motion blur, Gaussian noise and a combination of all. Face width decreases from top to bottom: 128, 64 and 32 pixels.

Unconstrained Environment

Unconstrained face image capturing leads to two principal challenges: variations in illumination and head pose. Illumination is largely addressed implicitly by the application of local features and their successors as face image descriptor because, for example, LBP are invariant to monotonic illumination changes in the image. In contrast, head pose is often handled explicitly, for example, by partial-least-squares methods [Li11a, Fis12], dictionary learning [Mud17], or normalization by appropriate warping and mirroring [Bäu10]. Face recognition solutions based on CNNs choose the implicit pose modeling through appropriate training data which resulted in satisfying results [KS16].

2.1.4 Retrieval

Because traditional image retrieval approaches, such as bag-of-words [Siv03], are difficult to adapt to the face domain [Wu11], video face retrieval remains a challenging task. The main reasons are the smooth appearance of faces where classical keypoint based descriptors, such as SIFT, tend to fail and the difficulty to compactly represent a face sequence. Thus, the usage of further information, such as user feedback [Smi11] or attribute based retrieval [Che13a], appears to be in the focus of current face retrieval work. The basic problem of designing video face retrieval systems achieving a high performance in a small retrieval time appears to attract little attention. Relevant work in that area includes compact sequence descriptors by frame clustering [Zha08a] or Fisher vectors [Par14], or speeding up the distance measure [Hua11]. In particular, it is worth noting that some face verification systems are inadequate for face retrieval because computationally expensive classifier training steps are part of each face descriptor comparison [Ber12, Li13, Wol11, Wol13].

2.1.5 Datasets

Because face recognition is a common and competitive research field, the amount of datasets is vast. Datasets can have different purposes such as comparing or training face recognition methods, or addressing novel challenges. Over the course of time, face recognition datasets became larger and less restricted regarding the capturing conditions. While early public face datasets, such as the AT&T [Sam94] or Weizmann [Ull92] face databases, contained only few images of a few dozen persons in strictly controlled illumination and frontal pose conditions, current datasets, such as the MS-Celeb-1M dataset [Guo16], include several hundreds of thousands persons and many million images in total. Capturing conditions were relaxed up to completely unrestricted settings as, for example, in the UnConstrained College Students (UCCS) Dataset [Bou17]. The addressing of increasingly difficult scenarios is also reflected in the repeatedly performed Face Recognition Vendor Tests of the US National Institute of Standards and Technology (NIST) [Bla01, Phi03, Phi07b, Gro10b, Gro13].

The wide availability of tagged face images through the internet massively boosted the number and size of face recognition datasets because highly automated collection and annotation of the face images is enabled. All these datasets reflect high-quality image recordings originating from professional celebrity shootings, user's profile pictures or selfies. Notably, the largest of these datasets are private datasets of large internet companies [Tai14, Sch15b] containing hundreds of millions face images.

Datasets reflecting the low-quality domain as targeted by this thesis are still rare and often publicly unavailable because of privacy reasons [Sta07, Bäu10]. The few exceptions are the ChokePoint [Won11], SCFace [Grg11] and UnConstrained College Students (UCCS) Dataset [Bou17]. Out of these, only ChokePoint is a video dataset and none is a real large-scale dataset suitable for training massive classifiers such as CNNs. The main reason is that labeling of low-quality face data is hard even for humans which requires an unreasonable manual effort to generate large numbers of ground truth annotated samples. Table 2.3 gives a comprehensive overview of 2D face recognition datasets for the visible spectrum. Because face datasets are quickly evolving, the most up-to-date resources on face recognition databases can usually be found online[1,2].

Table 2.3: Face recognition datasets by release year.

dataset	**public**	**video**	**surveillance-like**	**images**	**sequences**	**persons**
Weizmann Face Image Database [Ull92]	✓			2.0K	-	28
AT&T / ORL Database of Faces [Sam94]	✓			400	-	40
JAFFE Database [Lyo98]	✓			213	-	10
XM2VTSDB [Mes99]	✓	✓		-	2.4K	295
Extended Yale Face Database [Geo00]	✓			19K	-	39
FERET [Phi00]	✓			14K	-	1.2K

1 http://www.face-rec.org/databases/

2 https://www.kairos.com/blog/60-facial-recognition-databases

CMU Motion of Body (MoBo) Database [Gro01]	✓	✓		-	96	25
BioID Face Database [Jes01]	✓			1.5K	-	41
CMU PIE [Sim02]	✓			41K	-	68
Indian Face Database [Jai02]	✓			735	-	63
Honda/UCSD Video Database [Lee03, Lee05]	✓	✓		29K	92	35
Face in Action [Goh05]	✓	✓		1.2M	6.2K	238
NRC-IIT Facial Video Database [Gor05]	✓	✓		7.4K	24	10
Face Recognition Grand Challenge [Phi05]	✓			50K	-	-
Buffy Dataset [Eve06]	✓	✓		81K	3.6K	21
Labeled Faces in the Wild (LFW) [Hua07]	✓			13K	-	1.7K
Youtube Celebrities [Kim08]	✓	✓		300K	1.9K	47
Essex Face Recognition Data [Spa08]	✓			7.9K	-	395
Put Face Database [Kas08]	✓			10K	-	100
VidTIMIT [San09]	✓	✓		100K	430	43
MultiPIE [Gro10a]	✓			750K	-	337
FEI Face Database [Tho10]	✓			2.8K	-	200
MUCT Face Database [Mil10]	✓	✓		3.7K	751	276
YouTube Faces Database (YTF) [Wol11]	✓	✓		620K	3.4K	1.6K
ChokePoint [Won11]	✓	✓	✓	64K	1.3K	29
SCFace [Grg11]	✓		✓	4.0K	-	130
PubFig+10 [Kum11, Ort13]	✓			44K	-	210

MSRA-CFW [Zha12a]	✓			200K	-	1.6K
Sheffield Face Database [Wec12]	✓			575	-	20
TBBT+Buffy [Bäu13]	✓	✓		540K	9.3K	40
Movie Trailer Face Dataset [Ort13]	✓	✓		110K	4.5K	146
PaSC [Bev13]	✓	(✓)		9.4K	2.8K	293
Celebrity-1000 [Liu14]	✓	✓		2.3M	160K	1.0K
FaceScrub [Ng14]	✓			61K	-	530
Facebook DeepFace dataset [Tai14]				4.4M	-	4.0K
CASIA WebFace Database [Yi14]	✓			500K	-	11K
VGG Face [Par15]	✓			830K	-	2.6K
Google FaceNet dataset [Sch15b]				200M	-	8M
IJB-A [Kla15]	✓	(✓)		51K	5.6K	500
Accio [Gha15]	✓	✓		1.9M	23K	121
UMDFaces [Ban16]	✓			370K	-	8.5K
MegaFace v1 [KS16]	✓			1.0M	-	690K
MegaFace v2 [Nec16]	✓			4.7M	-	670K
MS-Celeb-1M [Guo16]	✓			10M	-	100K
UnConstrained College Students Dataset [Bou17]	✓		✓	34K	-	1.1K

2.2 Local Features

While there exists a large variety of possibilities to describe objects in images, a selected subset has established itself in the field of face recognition. In the case of unsupervised methods, handcrafted local features are a popular and successful choice. Local features describe either a region of an image or the area around a point. Feature extraction is then performed either in regions from a fixed grid [Aho06, Bäu10, Jab10, Zou07a], around fixed points [Zou07a, Sim13] or around previously detected face landmarks [Wu11]. Extraction around landmarks can have negative effects because the face shape is ignored and only the appearance is included [Zou07a].

- **Region-based** local features extract information by describing the occurring patterns inside the target region. A widespread local feature to describe face images are the Local Binary Patterns (LBP) [Aho06] because of its invariance to monotonic illumination changes as a result of using a central pixel value as reference. Options with better noise resistance are the LTP [Lia10], LDP [Jab10] or Histogram of Oriented Gradients (HOG) [Alb08]. The MCT [Fro04] feature has improved outlier resistance. In all these cases, the local feature is constructed by a histogram of the extracted patterns in the region. Another illumination-robust option is the Discrete Cosine Transform (DCT) [Eke06, Sta07, Bäu10] which involves a frequency analysis.
- **Point-based** local features describe the neighborhood of a selected point as discriminatively as possible. The popular and highly discriminative SIFT keypoint-descriptor can be applied by feature extraction from a dense grid [Sim15]. Another common choice are Gabor features [Yan04b, Xie06] motivated by their similarity to the mammalian visual cortex [Mar80].

In comparison to a direct usage of the raw or transformed pixel intensity vector, the local feature strategies are more robust to illumination changes and small misalignments [Zou07a].

Typically, point-based local features require denser extraction than region-based features leading to significantly larger image descriptors. Extracting many features can still make sense when selecting only the best ones afterwards, for example, by boosting [Zha04b, Zha05].

2.3 Convolutional Neural Networks

Neural networks have been existing for quite some time and have made several evolvements over time into the current state which is often referred to as deep learning because of the increasing number of layers [Sch15a]. In computer vision, neural networks had their wide breakthrough as Convolutional Neural Networks (CNNs) in the ImageNet Challenge [Den09] where images have to be classified into one of 1000 classes according to the image content. The first CNN approach to enter the challenge, AlexNet [Kri12], reduced the error by a significant margin compared to previous solutions. However, CNNs have existed since the 80s [LC89] and applications to face related tasks, especially face detection, go back into the 90s [Vai94, Gar02, Gar04, Cho05, Duf08].

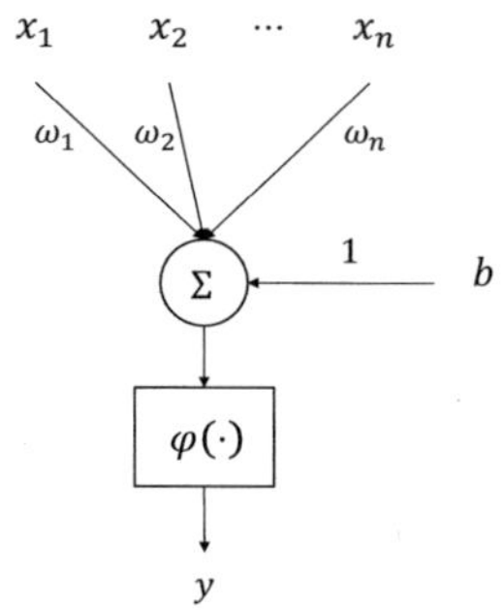

Figure 2.3: Perceptron structure.

Introduction

This section will losely follow the great and compact introduction to neural networks and CNNs by Zheng [Zhe16]. Deeper insights into the algorithms, theoretical capabilities and motivations are provided by Duda et al. [Dud01].

Neural networks consist of single neurons in the shape of perceptrons. This elementary neural unit has n scalar inputs resulting in an input vector $\boldsymbol{x} \in \mathbb{R}^n$ and one scalar output y as depicted in figure 2.3 [Ros58]. The output is the weighted sum of its inputs and a bias b:

$$y = \varphi\left(\boldsymbol{\omega}^T \boldsymbol{x} + b\right) . \tag{2.1}$$

The weight vector $\boldsymbol{\omega} \in \mathbb{R}^n$ consists of the input weights ω_i and φ is a non-linear function usually called the activation function. Common choices are the sigmoid function or especially for CNNs the Rectified Linear Unit (ReLU) activation function $\varphi(x) = \max(0,x)$ [Kri12].

Putting several perceptrons together, as illustrated in figure 2.4, is called a Multilayer Perceptron (MLP). It is a feedforward network of neuron layers where neurons of one layer are only connected with neurons from the previous and next layer but not within a layer. The output of the i-th layer is given by

$$\boldsymbol{h}_i = \varphi(W_i \boldsymbol{h}_{i-1} + \boldsymbol{b}_i) \tag{2.2}$$

with $\boldsymbol{h}_0 = \boldsymbol{x}$ being the input and $\boldsymbol{h}_N = \boldsymbol{y}$ being the output of an N-layer MLP. $W_i \in \mathbb{R}^{m \times n}$ is the layer's weight matrix with $W_i = [\boldsymbol{\omega}_{i1}, \ldots, \boldsymbol{\omega}_{im}]^T$ being the combined weight vectors of its m perceptrons. Together, all weight matrices W and bias vectors $\boldsymbol{b}$ are the trainable parameters of the network. With this pairwise connection of neurons between the layers, this layer type is also referred to as *fully connected layer*. Its number of parameters quickly rises with an increasing number of neurons in the network.

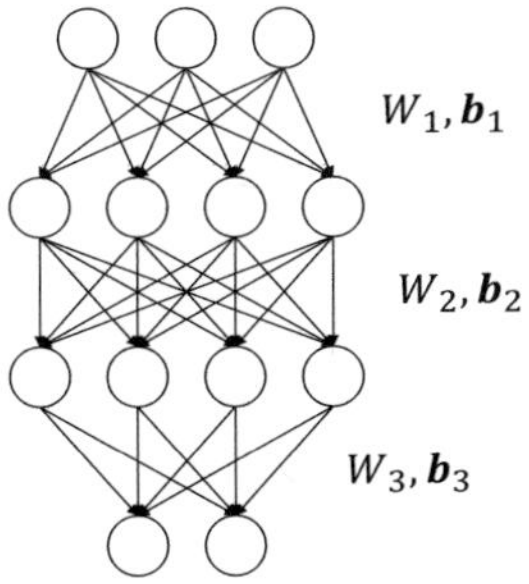

Figure 2.4: Multilayer Perceptron (MLP) structure.

Convolutional layers are a way to reduce the number of parameters by sparsity and regularization. Figure 2.5 illustrates both steps. First, by only connecting nearby neurons within a fixed spatial range, called the *receptive field*, from the previous layer as highlighted, the weight matrix becomes sparse. This type of sparse layer is known as *locally connected layer*. In the next step, the weights become independent of the position of the neuron, thus regularizing the remaining parameters of the weight matrix which then becomes a Toeplitz matrix. Convolutional layers are especially designed and used for either 1D or 2D signals with images being an example of the 2D case. This also explains the name of the convolutional layer because its parameters define a filter kernel with the size of the receptive field. The layer output is the convolution of the signal by this filter.

Networks which comprise at least one convolutional layer are called Convolutional Neural Networks (CNNs). A basic CNN consists of three key types of layers: convolutional, pooling and fully connected ones [LeC98]. Fully connected layers can be understood as classifiers and are usually put at the end of a CNN to classify the output of previous convolutional and pooling layers. These early layers in the CNN serve as a feature extractor. The convolutional kernel weights are learned and one convolutional layer applies multiple learned filters with the same $k \times k$ receptive field at once. This way, image structures such as edges or corners can be extracted. The result of one convolutional filter is usually referred to as *feature map*. When interpreting the input as an image, pooling layers group several pixels spatially and propagate, for example, only the mean or the maximum of a spatial region to the next layer. This includes a downsampling and serves to aggregate neighboring features, creating robustness to shift and distortion, and allows to extract increasingly abstract representations in the subsequent layers. Stacking up a set of alternating convolutional and pooling layers at the beginning and a few fully connected layers at the end of the network yields a basic CNN.

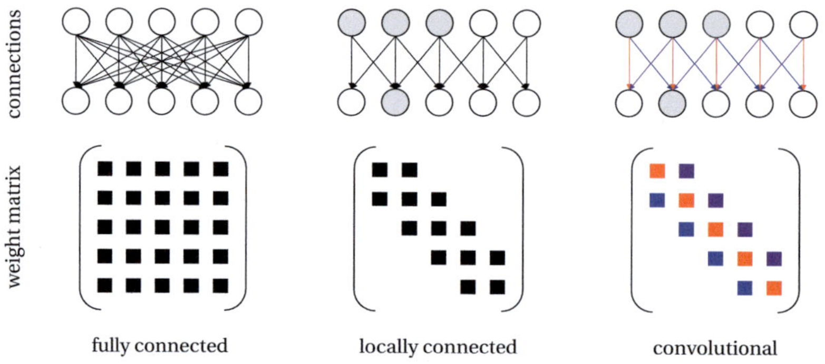

Figure 2.5: Transition from a fully connected to a 1D convolutional layer.

The network is learned in a supervised manner by back-propagation with a loss function L that formulates the desired outcome. A common optimization method is stochastic gradient descent where the gradient is determined for a small subset of the training data and then back-propagated through the network [Mon98]. The subset, which is usually called a batch $\mathcal{B}$, can be processed efficiently in one step on current GPU-hardware. A training step t is thus given by

$$W^{t+1} = W^t + \Delta\hat{W}^t \tag{2.3}$$

with

$$\Delta\hat{W}^t = \psi \sum_{x \in \mathcal{B}_t} \frac{\partial L_x}{\partial W} \tag{2.4}$$

being the gradient over the batch which is weighted by the learning rate ψ. Further tweaks to get faster convergence and less overfitting are momentum and weight decay. Momentum adds a portion α of the previous weight update to the current one in the update step of the stochastic gradient descent [Dud01]:

$$W^{t+1} = W^t + \Delta\hat{W}^t + \alpha\Delta\hat{W}^{t-1} \,. \tag{2.5}$$

This helps to overcome plateaus in the loss function. Weight decay additionally decreases the weights in each training step by a small amount ε [Dud01]

$$W^{\text{new}} = (1-\varepsilon) \cdot W^{\text{old}} \tag{2.6}$$

to avoid overfitting caused by overly large weights.

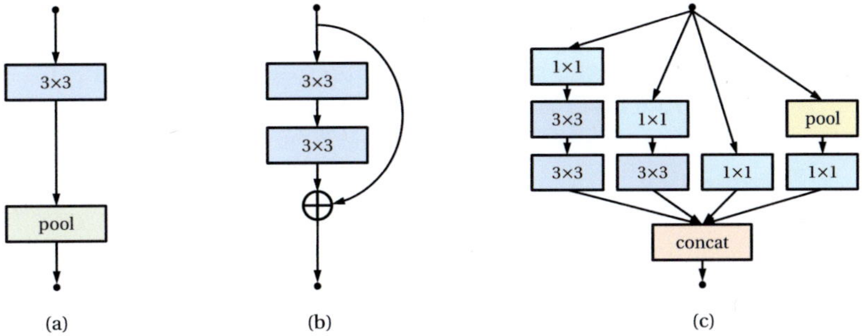

Figure 2.6: Key components for each architecture type. Alternating convolutional and pooling layers for classical type (a), residual block (b) and inception module (c).

Architecture

Since LeNet [LeC98] and AlexNet [Kri12], the key components of current CNNs have remained similar but different architecture arrangements were proposed to increase the performance. The currently most notable architectures are:

- An extension of the classical LeNet and AlexNet in the **VGG network** [Sim15] where several convolutional layers with small receptive fields replace a single layer with a large receptive field which allowed to increase the network depth up to 19 layers while limiting parameter growth to a reasonable extent.
- The **residual architecture** [He15a] adding a bypass of every two convolutional layers (figure 2.6b). By forwarding the identity, the network has to learn only a small residual modifying the identity which is supposed to lead to better trainability for very deep networks. Using this strategy, this architecture type currently allows the deepest networks with about 1000 layers in certain applications [He16]. A similar concept is proposed by the highway networks [Sri15].
- The **inception architecture** [Sze15b] introducing a special kind of meta layer called inception module (figure 2.6c). It is composed of a specific parallel arrangement of convolutional and pooling layers motivated by multi-scale processing. Efficient usage of computing resources is implemented by 1×1 convolutional layers which reduce data dimension.

Network Types and Loss Functions

A network architecture can be applied for differing tasks depending on the design of the output layer and the loss function. The two relevant options for face recognition are classification and verification.

- **Classification**. The input should be categorized into one of N_{out} classes which is reflected by an output layer with N_{out} neurons. The most well-known examples are the networks designed for the ImageNet Challenge [Kri12, Sim15, Sze15b, He15a, He16] which have 1000 output neurons, one for each of the 1000 object categories of the challenge. A lot of face recognition networks also follow this principle [Tai14, Par15, Wen16] with each identity in the training data being a class. The number of output neurons thus depends on the training dataset and is typically in the range of a few thousand. Typical loss function: Softmax [Dud01] or center loss [Wen16].

- **Verification**. The input is projected into a low-dimensional discriminative target space forcing a desired relation between input pairs such as a low distance. This can be seen as task specific dimension reduction or metric learning [Zhe16]. The output layer has as many neurons as the desired target space has dimensions. This is especially useful for open-set face recognition [Sch15b, Din16b]. Typical loss function: contrastive [Had06] or triplet loss [Sch15b, Din16b].

Network Details

A lot of detail concepts are necessary to make deep CNNs work. This includes choosing the ReLU activation function instead of a sigmoid one to save runtime and avoid vanishing gradients [Kri12]. An improved ReLU version allows faster convergence of the network training by using a small slope for values below zero instead of a constant output [He15b]. Proper initialization of network weights is important to avoid vanishing or exploding gradient issues in networks with many layers. The initial weights for a layer are sampled from a zero-mean Gaussian distribution with a variance dependent on the layer's size and the applied activation function [Glo10, He15b]. An additional option to normalize value range for faster learning is batch normalization where network activations are normalized to zero mean and unit variance after each weight layer by

$$\boldsymbol{h}_i = \alpha_i \boldsymbol{h}_{i-1} + \beta_i \tag{2.7}$$

with layer-wise learned parameters α and β [Iof15]. Batch normalization is required to reliably train very deep architectures such as the inception or residual one.

Data Augmentation

The generalization capabilities of machine learning systems, with CNNs being no expection, increase with the variety of training data presented to the system. With access to private very large-scale datasets containing up to several hundred million face images relying simply on the vast amount of data can be an option for big companies [Sch15b, Tai14]. If limited to smaller public datasets [Par15, Guo16, Liu14, Nec16, Ng14, Yi14, Zha12a] usually containing less or slightly above one million face images, data augmentation strategies [Mas16] can compensate for the lack of data. Parkhi et al. applied different crops and flipping to train their face network [Par15]. Their strategy is probably motivated by the common training strategies for the ImageNet Challenge which apply cropping, flipping and color shift to improve the results [Sim15, Kri12]. For low-quality data from the surveillance domain, results for the person re-identification scenario indicate that different crops, flipping and rotation are helpful, while color changes or affine transformations tend to decrease the results [McL15]. Regarding data quality, training on artificially blurred imagery improves recognition performance on video data captured with handheld devices [Din16b].

3 Concept

Starting from the raw video, figure 3.1 illustrates the face detection, tracking and alignment stages. They are out of the scope of this thesis and are considered as preprocessing steps. By these steps, invariance to in-plane rotation, scaling and shifting is achieved in principle. However, no perfect alignment is assumed and accordingly tolerant methods are proposed to additionally improve the robustness. Given an aligned set of tracked face sequences, also referred to as face tracks, the scope of this thesis is to efficiently represent these tracks in an index database to enable fast and accurate face search given unseen query sequences.

This task involves two key parts. First, the representation of a single face image by an appropriate descriptor and, second, the combination of a sequence of face image descriptors into the face sequence descriptor. Because this thesis targets video data, the low data quality caused by the surveillance domain can be counteracted by fusing temporal information across consecutive face samples. This might increase the observed articulation variety of a face by including different occurring aspects such as head pose, illumination or expression. The proposed and analyzed methods in this work are particularly designed for low-quality unconstrained video-to-video face verification and retrieval. The data is restricted to the common 2D case and the visible color spectrum.

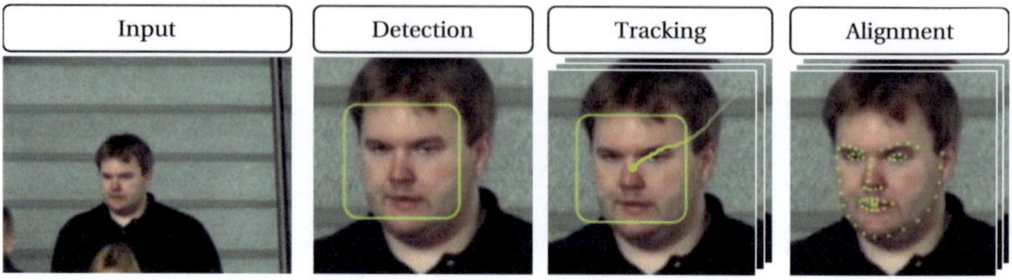

Figure 3.1: Preprocessing: creating face tracks.

A key challenge for practical applications is the generalization capability, especially with the wide variety of data quality in the addressed case of surveillance footage. Thus, two different approaches are explored:

- An unsupervised strategy based on handcrafted local features and the bag-of-words approach which both require no external training data. Because no domain overfitting can occur, this is expected to generalize well to unseen data.
- A supervised strategy leveraging public large-scale face datasets as training data to learn an improved CNN-based face descriptor suitable for low-resolution applications coupled with a center-based sequence descriptor. Because of the exploitation of external training data, it is expected to be superior in scenarios similar to the training data but it is also inherently prone to overfitting to this data. Methods to counteract this effect are proposed and analyzed with respect to the achieved level of generalization.

The final comparison and evaluation of both approaches is performed on surveillance-like public video datasets as well as on self-collected actual surveillance video footage. Before presenting both concepts, the addressed tasks of face verification and face retrieval will be specified more formally.

3.1 Face Verification

Given a sequence $T = (\boldsymbol{u}_1, \dots, \boldsymbol{u}_n)$ of aligned face image vectors $\boldsymbol{u}_i$, a face sequence descriptor $\mathcal{W}$ is a unified representation of these face images allowing face comparison. In order to extract $\mathcal{W}$, each face image $\boldsymbol{u}$ is first described by a face image descriptor $\mathcal{V}$ using a face descriptor method $\mathcal{C} : \boldsymbol{u} \mapsto \mathcal{V}$. Then, the sequence of face image descriptors is mapped to the sequence descriptor $(\mathcal{V}_1, \dots, \mathcal{V}_n) \mapsto \mathcal{W}$. Given two face tracks T_1, T_2, face verification decides if both samples show the same person identity C, as illustrated in figure 3.2. More formally, face verification decides if $\mathcal{I}(T_1) = \mathcal{I}(T_2)$, where $\mathcal{I}$ denotes the function assigning the person identity C to a sample: $\mathcal{I} : T_i \mapsto C_i$. In the verification process, the face sequence descriptors $\mathcal{W}_1, \mathcal{W}_2$ are determined and compared regarding their similarity. Often, the similarity score $\mathcal{S}(\mathcal{W}_1, \mathcal{W}_2) \in \mathbb{R}$ is either the negative or inverse distance $\mathcal{D}(\mathcal{W}_1, \mathcal{W}_2)$ between the sequence descriptors using an appropriate distance measure $\mathcal{D}$.

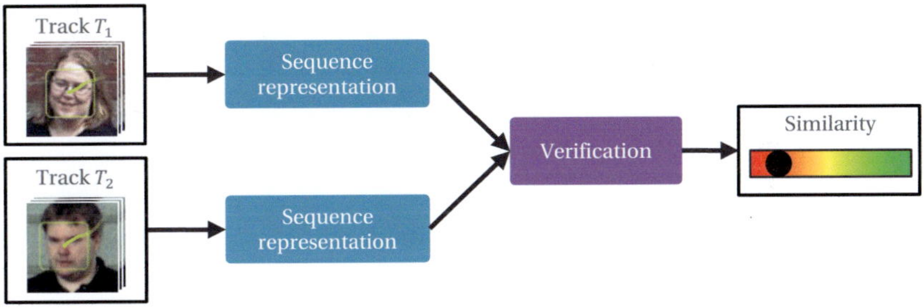

Figure 3.2: Face verification overview.

3.2 Face Retrieval

Face retrieval is the task of searching faces in a prepared index database of face descriptors $\mathcal{W}_i$ (figure 3.3). Given a query sequence T_q, the database sequences with matching identity $\mathcal{I}(T_q) = C_q$ are to be found. In applications where retrieval tasks occur, it is unnecessary to make a hard decision. Instead, it is sufficient to list the N database sequences in a ranking Q_q of results sequences T_s ordered by the similarity score $\mathcal{S}$ indicating the likelihood of showing the same identity C_q as the query track T_q:

$$Q_q = \left(T_{s_1}, \ldots, T_{s_N}\right), \quad s_i \neq s_j \text{ for } i \neq j \text{ and } \mathcal{S}\left(\mathcal{W}_{s_i}, \mathcal{W}_q\right) \geq \mathcal{S}\left(\mathcal{W}_{s_{i+1}}, \mathcal{W}_q\right) .$$

In the end, the ranking serves for manual inspection by a human operator extracting the relevant information.

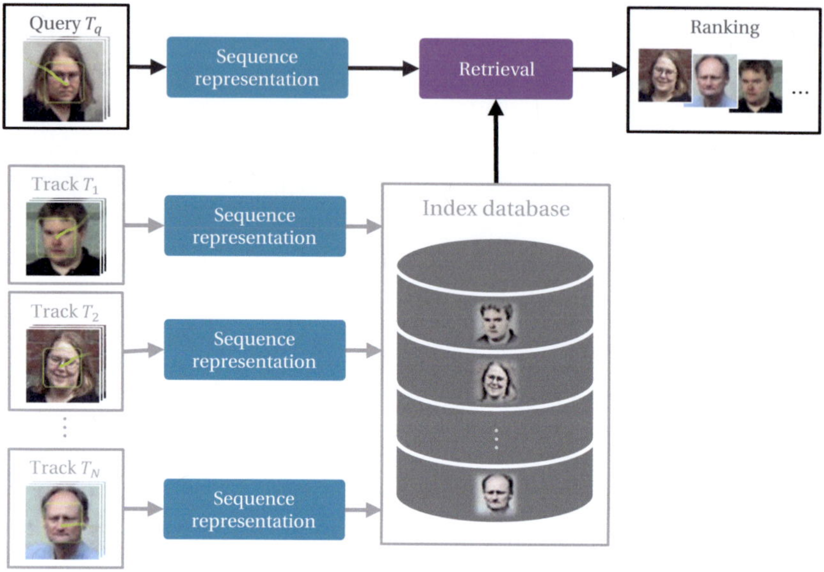

Figure 3.3: Face retrieval overview.

3.3 Unsupervised Method

The first explored method is based on a completely unsupervised processing chain which is motivated by the implicit robustness to domain changes. Face images are described by a low-resolution adjusted LBP descriptor, exploiting multi-scale information to create dense feature histograms despite the sparse data [Her13a]. The reasons to choose LBP as local feature include

- its invariance to monotonic illumination changes which helps to address the unconstrained capturing conditions,
- the easy adaptation of local patch sizes and shapes in contrast to SIFT, for example, and
- the robustness to pixel shift, because of the histogram.

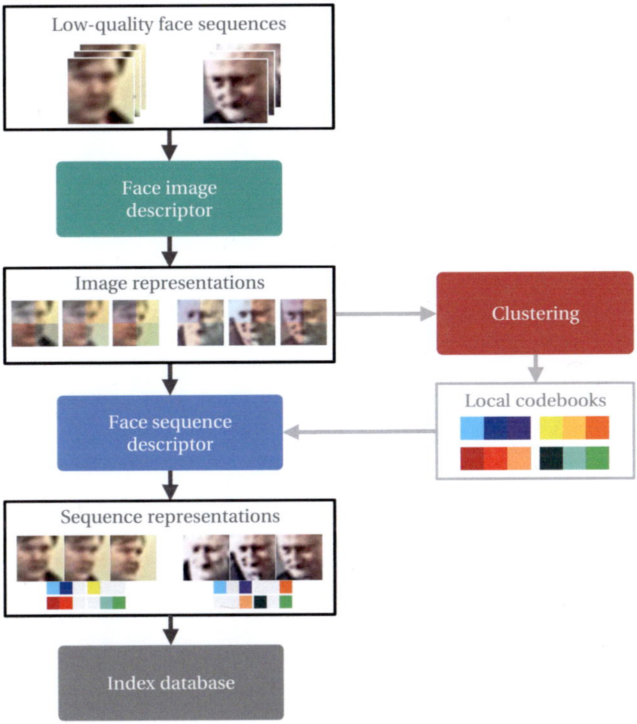

Figure 3.4: Data indexing concept for the local feature-based unsupervised strategy.

The applied sequence descriptor depends on the task in this case.

- Face verification can be performed based on common set- or space-based sequence descriptors as presented in section 2.1.2. An efficient choice is, for example, MSM [Fuk05].
- Face retrieval is performed by a bag-of-words-based strategy known from image retrieval methods [Siv03]. This cumulative descriptor builds the sequence model out of the set of local features from one face sequence. It consists of a list of present visual words. The code-book of possible visual words is learned in an unsupervised way from the set of database face sequences so neither external nor annotated training data is required. For fast and accurate search, an adapted inverted index approach is proposed (section 5.2.3). One reason why

this bag-of-words strategy was previously unsuccessful is the comparison of local features from different locations in the face to each other. Two options solving this issue are proposed and explored. First, local inverted indices to assert that only features from the same location in the face will be compared [Her15b] (illustrated in figure 3.4). Second, feature augmentation by concatenation of the local feature vector and a unique feature location encoding vector for better local aggregation of features into visual words during codebook generation [Her15a].

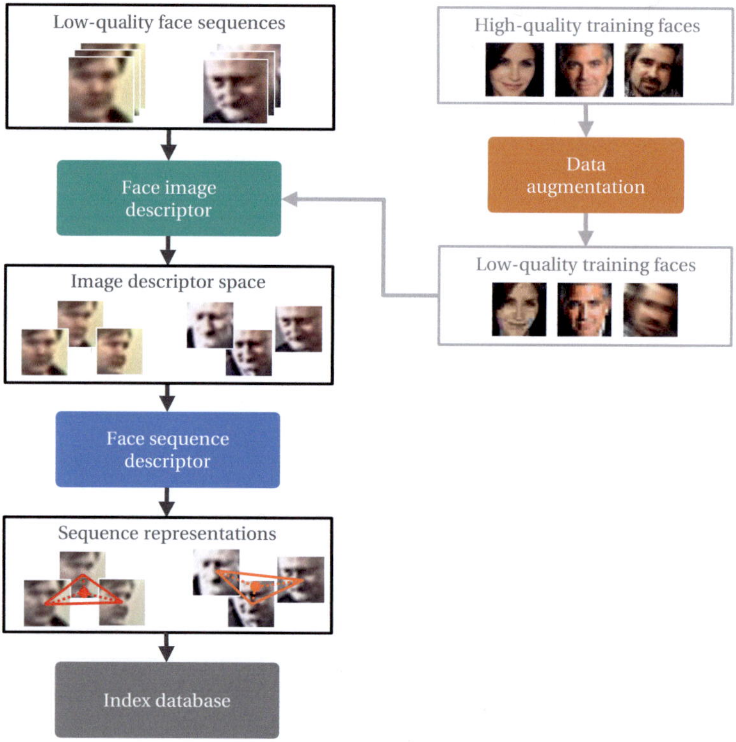

Figure 3.5: Data indexing concept for the CNN-based supervised strategy.

3.4 Supervised Method

An effective CNN-based descriptor is proposed which proves to be more efficient compared to previous solutions and addresses domain shift by training data augmentation. Temporal information is employed to build a noise resistant sequence descriptor. Figure 3.5 shows the proposed system consisting of the CNN to extract face image descriptors and the center-based face sequence descriptor.

Face Image Descriptor

The CNN-based low-quality optimized face image descriptor is trained on external data which makes this strategy a supervised one. In general, a significant amount of work on CNNs is based on transfer learning in the shape of fine-tuning pretrained networks for the task at hand. Face recognition methods are no exception [Par15, Wu16]. However, networks are usually pretrained with the ImageNet data [Den09] resulting in an input image size of typically 224×224 pixels which is only viable for HR applications. One option to leverage these networks for LR face recognition is the combination of a super resolution upscaling network and a HR network fine-tuned for face recognition [Wu16].

In contrast, the proposed method in this thesis follows the option of directly training a LR CNN from scratch which promises compacter and faster networks because it avoids the time consuming image upscaling and works on lower dimensional input [Her16c]. Similar to [Cho05, Sch15b], the proposed verification network $\mathcal{C}$ maps the input face image $\boldsymbol{u}$ to a discriminative target vector space with Euclidean distance being meaningful for face similarity: $\mathcal{C}(\boldsymbol{u}) = \boldsymbol{v}$ and $\mathcal{D}(\mathcal{V}_1, \mathcal{V}_2) = ||\boldsymbol{v}_1 - \boldsymbol{v}_2||_2$. This is achieved by a Siamese *verification* training setup [Bro94] having three key advantages compared with a *classification* strategy:

- The descriptor dimension, which equals the number of neurons in the output layer, is independent of the number of person identities in the dataset and can be chosen arbitrarily. In practice, this allows smaller descriptors $\boldsymbol{v}$.
- It directly models the comparison task in the network leading to a better control over the distance.
- It allows to combine several training datasets without any effort because no consistent identity labels between datasets are required.

Three different state-of-the-art architecture types (inception [Sch15b], residual [He15a] and classical [Par15]) are selected as base for the CNN face image descriptor and explored with regard to their suitability for LR face matching (section 4.2.1). A structural analysis of the architectures is performed to determine the necessary adjustments and potential bottlenecks of the networks for the LR task. Architecture meta-parameters such as number and type of layers are systematically optimized to identify the best configuration (section 6.3.1). A max-margin-based loss instead of the common contrastive or triplet losses is applied for more efficient network training [Her16c].

To address the low data quality, novel training data augmentation strategies are proposed in section 4.2.2. Besides common geometric augmentations such as flipping, cropping and rotation [Par15, McL15], quality related augmentations namely adding noise, motion blur or compression artifacts, and rescaling are employed [Her16b]. This is necessary to train on sufficiently large-scale face datasets [Guo16, Liu14, Nec16, Ng14, Par15, Yi14, Zha12a] which are non-surveillance high-quality datasets and consequently involve a domain gap to the targeted low-quality surveillance footage.

Face Sequence Descriptor

Regarding the face sequence descriptor, previous work on CNN face image descriptors applied the *set-based* pair-wise comparison of face image descriptors [Sch15b, Tai14, Par15]. This strategy has been shown to be effective [Che11b, Wol11], but is highly inefficient due to its $\mathcal{O}\left(n^2\right)$ complexity. Thus, the key concept of the proposed face track comparison method is to keep the effectiveness while significantly increasing the efficiency. Even though options to speed up pair-wise comparison of set-based face sequence descriptors in retrieval scenarios have been explored [Her14b], it is preferable to have a compact sequence descriptor in the beginning. A center-based strategy is proposed and motivated by observations about the face image descriptor space and compactness considerations about the applied max-margin loss function.

3.5 Domain Specific Data

As already covered in table 2.3, the number of face video datasets is significantly smaller than the number of face image datasets and in most cases the dataset size is limited. Two strategies to compensate for this lack of data are followed. First, CNN network training data is enhanced by large-scale public face image datasets to enlarge the data variety. Second, two face datasets are collected, one suitable for training, the other for testing on surveillance domain faces.

Large-Scale Face Video Dataset: TVC

Large-scale video datasets including a sufficient amount of persons and sequences to train complex models, such as CNNs, are rare. Known options are the Celebrity-1000 [Liu14] and to some extent the Accio [Gha15] dataset. Their drawback is the partial identity overlap with other popular evaluation datasets such as YTF [Wol11] which has to be handled for proper separation of training and test data. Thus for training large-scale models, a novel dataset is collected from TV-recordings [Her15a, Her16c]. Special care is taken to select only local productions from German public broadcasting stations (mainly ARD and ZDF) where none of the celebrities from common public datasets occur. Consequently, Hollywood movies or news shows are excluded to avoid any identity overlap.

A mixture of 57 different recordings including movies, series, talk shows and documentaries is collected. Faces are tracked by a Viola-Jones-based face tracker [Vio04] and aligned by normalizing eye locations [Qu15]. False-positives are automatically removed by a second plausibility stage looking for skin color and sufficient visible face parts (at least two out of both eyes, nose and mouth), similar to [Tap14]. The remaining face tracks are labeled semi-automatically by using track aggregation with the VGG Face descriptor [Par15] and meta-data such as movie actor lists. Several persons appear in multiple recordings which increases the face appearance variety of the included persons. Especially in case of actors playing different characters, facial variations such as different hair style and color are covered. Altogether, 25,619 sequences with an average of 73.4 frames from 628 persons are included in this TV Collection (TVC) dataset. The overall data quality is comparable to Celebrity-1000 or YTF which means it is somewhere in between the high-quality single image data such as included in the LFW [Hua07] or FaceScrub [Ng14] dataset and low-quality surveillance footage.

Figure 3.6: Frame and face samples from the IOSB-SURV footage. Each row shows a different location, columns show variety at the respective location.

Low-Quality Face Video Dataset: IOSB-SURV

Collecting the TVC dataset still leaves the task how to properly address the actual target scenario of low-quality surveillance footage. Again, public datasets are of no significant help in this case. The single established video dataset collected under surveillance conditions is the ChokePoint dataset [Won11]. Besides being rather small with only 29 persons, the cameras were positioned strategically in the tight hallways so that people had to walk by closely. This results in a few frames for each face track with high image quality and a rather large face size mostly exceeding 100×100 pixels.

To better represent the target scenario, a large in-the-wild surveillance dataset called IOSB-SURV is collected from video data recorded at different occasions [Her17]. This includes the public portion of the data in shape of the SoBiS dataset [Sch14] as well as several internal data recordings. The data was recorded over the course of several years at three different sites across the city with outdoor scenes from all sites and indoor scenes from two sites, as illustrated in figure 3.6. The data includes day and night scenes from several cameras per location. A large variety of cameras was present, including actual on-site surveillance cameras. Again, faces are tracked by the Viola-Jones-based face tracker, aligned by eye locations and manually labeled resulting in a dataset size of 5,011 face tracks of 138 persons. The median face width is 50.3 pixels and the track length varies from 14 to over 2,100 frames with an average length of 73.2 frames.

Statistics for both self-collected datasets are given in table 3.1. Figure 3.7 indicates the differences in face size distributions between high-quality and surveillance, as well as the collected and comparative publicly available datasets. Regarding the difference between the collected IOSB-SURV and the public ChokePoint surveillance datasets, the median over the largest faces per track is 57.3 pixels for IOSB-SURV while it is 129.3 pixels for ChokePoint even though the face size distribution on frame level is rather similar. This makes ChokePoint a significantly easier face dataset, because high-quality face samples are available for most sequenceswhereas IOSB-SURV contains a lot of sequences consisting only of low-quality face images.

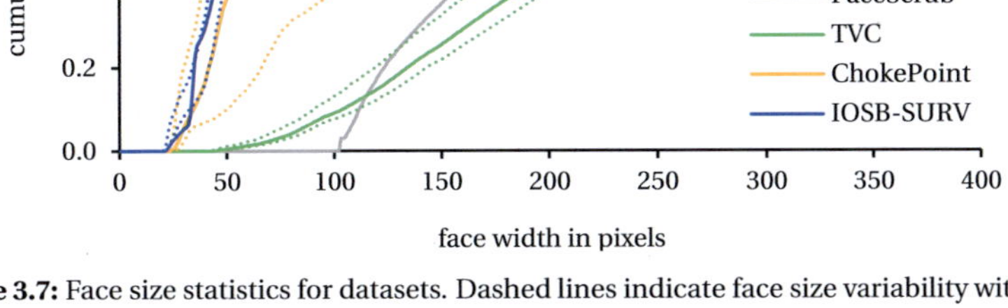

Figure 3.7: Face size statistics for datasets. Dashed lines indicate face size variability within a sequence for video datasets by the size distribution of the smallest and largest face per track.

Table 3.1: Self-collected face recognition datasets.

dataset	**public**	**video**	**surveillance**	**images**	**sequences**	**persons**
TVC		✓		1.8M	26K	628
IOSB-SURV	(✓)	✓	✓	370K	5K	138

4 Face Image Representation

As presented in the previous chapter, a face image vector $\boldsymbol{u}$ is described by a face image descriptor $\mathcal{V}$ using a method $\mathcal{C} : \boldsymbol{u} \mapsto \mathcal{V}$. In the following sections both proposed options, the unsupervised [Her13a, Her15a] and the supervised one [Her16c, Her16b], will be presented and discussed in detail.

4.1 Unsupervised: Local Features

For local matching, the face image is divided into $N = l_w \times l_h$ regions with each region being represented by a local region feature [Zou07a]. Usually, the local feature vectors of all regions are concatenated and serve as descriptor $\mathcal{V}$ for the whole face:

$$\mathcal{V} = \boldsymbol{v} = \begin{pmatrix} \boldsymbol{h}_1 \\ \vdots \\ \boldsymbol{h}_N \end{pmatrix}, \tag{4.1}$$

for region features $\boldsymbol{h}_i$, as illustrated in figure 4.1.

To represent face images in an unsupervised way, a handcrafted local feature is required to describe the local regions. LBP-based features are proven to be suitable for face recognition [Aho04, Aho06, Zou07a] and show several conceptual benefits. The key aspect is the possibility to address low-resolution face recognition by allowing small regions. In addition, its invariance to monotonic illumination changes and its fast computation are desirable for face recognition applications.The LBP extraction at a pixel is illustrated in figure 4.2: the neighborhood pixel intensities are thresholded and the result is interpreted as binary and subsequently decimal pattern [Oja02]. Uniform patterns denoted as LBP^{u2}, reduce the number of possible patterns by aggregating all noise patterns into a single pattern. All binary patterns showing more than two 0/1 or 1/0 changes are considered as noise patterns which significantly reduces the number of patterns (table 4.1). Pattern extraction is also possible beyond the strict 8-neighborhood. As presented in [Oja02], a circular neighborhood with varying radius r and number of neighbor points p is possible where pixel intensities are interpolated for off-grid points (figure 4.3a). Such a pattern is called $LBP^{u2}_{p,r}$.

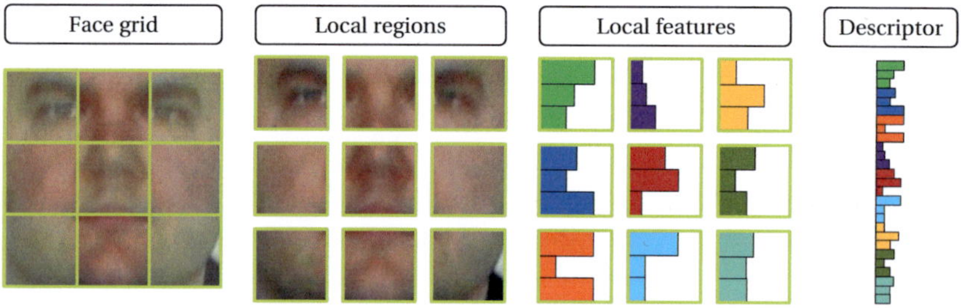

Figure 4.1: Face image descriptor extraction.

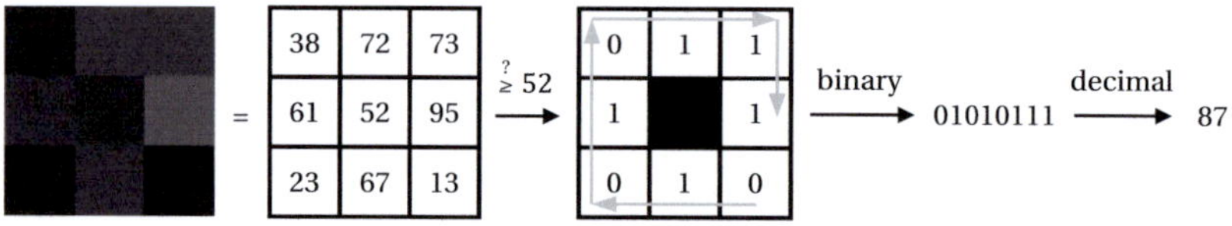

Figure 4.2: Basic LBP extraction according to [Aho06].

Table 4.1: Number of uniform LBP-histogram bins B for a given number of neighbors p.

p	4	6	8	10	12
B	15	33	59	93	135

Accumulation of the LBPs of an image region in a histogram yields a local region feature $\boldsymbol{h}$. Descriptor similarity can be measured by χ^2- [Aho06] or Hellinger-distance [Wol08, Ara12d].

The challenges of local matching for LR face images arise with the parameter choice. A common choice for HR faces are $LBP^{u2}_{8,2}$ patterns and a division of the face in 7×7 regions [Aho06, Zou07a]. Assuming a typical LR face image size of 28×28 pixels, using 7×7 regions would result in a region width of 4 pixels. This is already smaller than the $LBP_{8,2}$ operator which has a width of 5 pixels. Reducing the number of regions will solve this problem, but another one remains: the LBP histograms are very sparse. Sticking to a local approach, at least 2×2 regions are necessary leading to only 100 patterns within one region. Being distributed among 59 histogram bins, this can be sufficient, but it is desirable to increase the number of regions as far as possible without creating sparse histograms.

Consequently a trade-off between many fine-granular local regions, which are desirable to better capture local facial features, and large local regions leading to dense histograms has to be made. This leads to the curve depicted in figure 4.5 in green, where trade-off points can be chosen from. Higher face resolution obviously leads to a better curve (red). The following section proposes a solution to obtain a better trade-off curve without the necessity of a higher face resolution by addressing the sparsity issue.

4.1.1 Multi-Scale Histogram Fusion

There exist two principle ways to populate the local LBP histograms $\boldsymbol{h}$ with patterns: reduce the number of histogram bins leading to more patterns per bin, or increase the overall number of patterns [Her13a]. The number of bins B depends on the number of neighbors p a pattern is built of. For uniform patterns there are

$$B = p(p-1) + 3 \tag{4.2}$$

histogram bins because the binary pattern is only allowed to have one continuous sequence of ones, as illustrated in figure 4.3b. Thus, there are p positions where the sequence begins and $p-1$ different lengths. The three fixed bins are all-zeros, all-ones and non-uniform patterns. Table 4.1 shows the number of histogram bins for uniform patterns for different choices of p. Instead of decreasing the number of bins which reduces discrimination power, it is preferable to fill the histogram with more patterns. This improves the ability to distinguish between more individual texture details of the face.

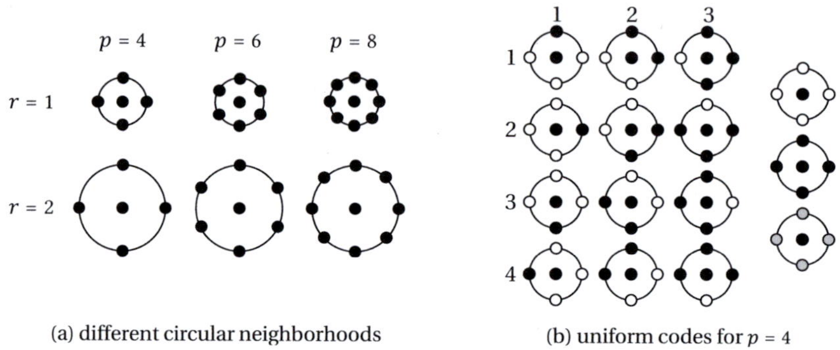

Figure 4.3: Details about LBP configurations.

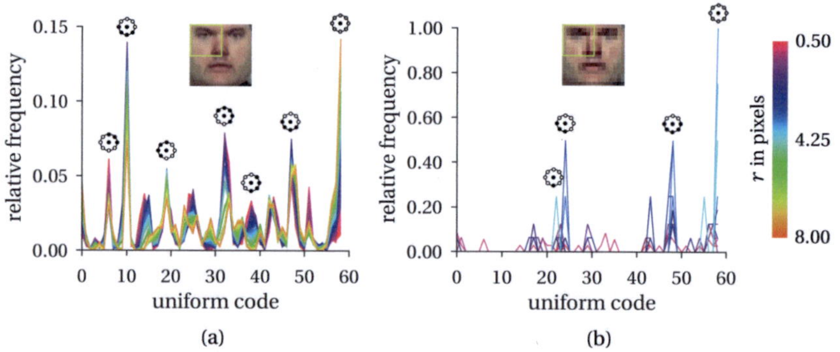

Figure 4.4: Overlay of $LBP^{u2}_{8,r}$ histograms for different radius choices. Comparison for a large 64 × 64 pixels (a) and small 8 × 8 pixels (b) version of the same image region.

Additional patterns can be created by extraction at different scales. Dense histograms are created by histogram fusion across different radii r_i within the same region:

$$\boldsymbol{h}_{\text{dense}} = \sum_i \boldsymbol{h}_i. \tag{4.3}$$

Since the neighborhood intensity values can be interpolated, it is possible to choose non-integer radii r_i. However, histograms $\boldsymbol{h}_i$ from different radii r_i become more similar with decreasing radius differences and decreasing region size, as indicated in figure 4.4. Despite the small radius sampling step of merely 0.01 pixels, all histograms for the 64 × 64 pixels HR version of this region are unique. For the downsampled 8 × 8 pixels LR case, only 12 percent of the histograms are unique, indicating that overly dense radius sampling is unnecessary in this case. It is also evident that histogram fusion reduces sparsity by creating an implicit statistic about the occurrence frequency of each uniform pattern across different scales.

Assuming a square local region of fixed width w, the number of patterns n_r of radius r is:

$$n_r = (\max(w - 2 \cdot \lceil r \rceil, 0))^2. \tag{4.4}$$

LBPs for positions at the border of the region drop out if their neighborhood lies partially outside the region. Thus, with increasing radius r, the number of patterns in a histogram decreases. Using several different radii r_i increases the total number n of available patterns to:

$$n = \sum_i n_{r_i}. \tag{4.5}$$

Depending on the number of applied scales for the strategy, this can create histograms as dense as for a multiple of the original face resolution which is illustrated in figure 4.5.

A key benefit of this LR-LBP strategy with regard to large-scale face retrieval is the unchanged dimension d of the final face image descriptor, leading to an unchanged comparison effort. Altogether, only a limited set of metaparameters has to be optimized, namely the number of regions via l_w and l_h, the number of neighbors p, and the number and size of radii r_i.

4.1.2 Multi-Scale Region Extraction

Region extraction can extend beyond the $l_w \times l_h$ regions in the input image. Additional regions can be extracted by introducing a region overlap ζ for denser region sampling and an image pyramid for additional scales [Her15d]. Usually, an image pyramid consists of multiple scales that differ by a constant scaling factor $0 < \lambda < 1$, thus the face scale recursion is $\hat{w}_{n+1} = \lambda \cdot \hat{w}_n$

for the face width $\hat{w}$. Face height $\hat{h}$ behaves analogously. The region size is kept constant, thus on higher scales with $\hat{w}_i < \hat{w}_0$ less than $l_w \times l_h$ regions will be extracted if the region overlap becomes too large. The drawback of this multi-scale strategy compared to the histogram fusion is that each additional region histogram from further scales increases the final face image descriptor size d.

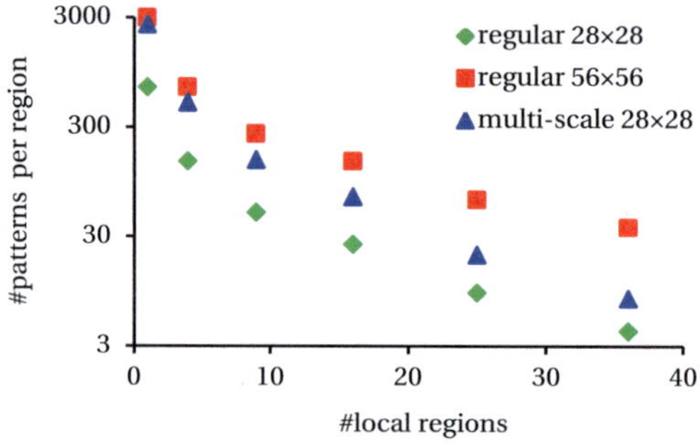

Figure 4.5: Comparison of a 4-scale fusion strategy ($r = \frac{1}{2}, 1, \frac{3}{2}, 2$) with regular LBP histogram extraction in terms of histogram density.

4.1.3 Feature Augmentation by Meta-Data

When collecting local features to describe an object by cumulative descriptors, it was proven useful to augment the feature by its image coordinates [Li13, Par14, Sim13]. This concatenation of a feature vector and its image coordinates improves face recognition because cumulative descriptors have no implicit feature location representation in contrast to feature concatenation, for example. Because feature location is obviously important to match faces to avoid comparing eye features with mouth features, location augmentation reintroduces this information into cumulative descriptors.

The proposed sequence descriptor strategy, which will be presented in section 5.2, is based on a cumulative bag-of-words descriptor [Siv03], which is why a mechanism to reintroduce feature location is required. Feature augmentation addresses this on feature level. An improved strategy addressing this on sequence descriptor level will be presented later in section 5.2.3. Because the feature augmentation by location encodes the measurement conditions of the feature only partially, an extended augmentation strategy by head pose is proposed [Her15a]. It is shown that the combination of location and head pose uniquely encodes the geometric measurement conditions of the respective local feature, thus creating a theoretical foundation for this strategy.

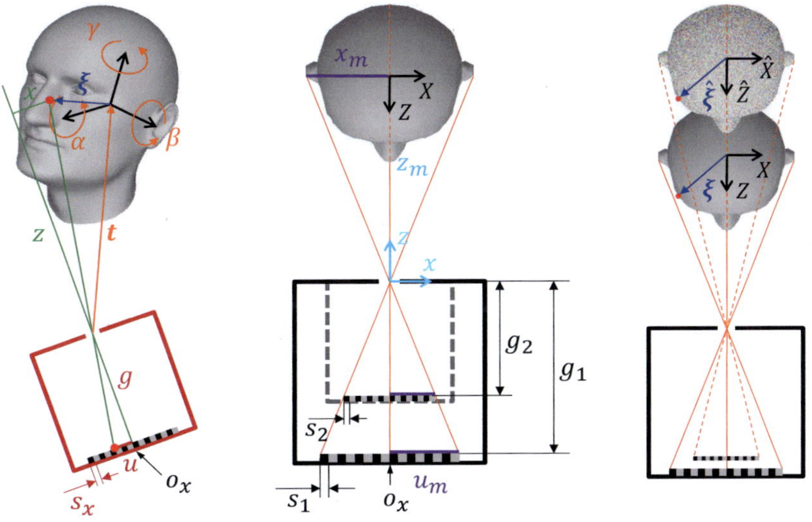

(a) (b) (c)

Figure 4.6: Illustration of the recording situation: (a) all measurement parameters, including global target position (blue), head position (orange), local target position (green) and camera parameters (red), (b) virtual sensor orientation and its pixel size adaptation, (c) virtual sensor is invariant to object distance.

Each local feature is captured under specific measurement conditions, originating from different positions in the face and from different viewing angles caused by unconstrained head motion and camera position. Figure 4.6a gives an overview of the characteristic parameters including head shape, position and camera parameters (pinhole camera), which have to be determined. First, a measurement targets a specific location $\boldsymbol{\xi} = (X,Y,Z)^T$ on the head or face and secondly, three rotation angles α, β, γ and a translation vector $\boldsymbol{t}$ describe the relative position of head and camera. Finally, the intrinsic camera parameters of a pinhole camera are given by the distance g of the sensor from the projection center, the pixel scale $(s_x, s_y)^T$ and the sensor origin $(o_x, o_y)^T$. The camera calibration equations include the relations between all the parameters. Given the global coordinates $\boldsymbol{\xi} = (X, Y, Z)^T$ of a measurement, its camera coordinates are given by

$$\begin{pmatrix} x \\ y \\ z \end{pmatrix} = R \begin{pmatrix} X \\ Y \\ Z \end{pmatrix} + \boldsymbol{t}, \tag{4.6}$$

where $R = R_\alpha R_\beta R_\gamma$ denotes the rotation matrix. Using the camera coordinates $(x, y, z)^T$, the image coordinates $(u, v)^T$ are

$$\begin{pmatrix} u \\ v \end{pmatrix} = -\frac{g}{z} \begin{pmatrix} s_x^{-1} x \\ s_y^{-1} y \end{pmatrix} + \begin{pmatrix} o_x \\ o_y \end{pmatrix}. \tag{4.7}$$

The global coordinate system is assumed to be identical to the local head coordinate system to ease presentation. The knowledge of the head pose, given by α, β and γ, and the image coordinates $(u, v)^T$ suffices to uniquely identify the target location $\boldsymbol{\xi}$ on the head because of four observations:

1. **Face detection and alignment** enforce that the origin of the global coordinate system lies on the z-axis of a virtual camera coordinate system, which means $\boldsymbol{t} \approx (0, 0, z_0)^T$. This defines a virtual camera, which is directly pointed at the head. Face scaling to $\hat{w} \times \hat{h}$ pixels, which is a part of face alignment, results in a unified pixel scaling factor $s = s_x = s_y$, a constant sensor origin $o_x, o_y = const$ and, because of face registration, fixed image coordinates of the face boundary, denoted by $(u_m, v_m)^T = const$. This can be understood as taking the image by a virtual sensor with the resolution of $w_I \times h_I$ pixels which fits the scaling s exactly to match the size of the light rays of the face boundary, as shown in figure 4.6b.
2. **A constant head size** can be assumed in good approximation for all persons, at least for adults. According to [Bal10] head width is 154 ± 6mm (mean$\pm$*std*) and head height 199 ± 7mm for Caucasian, and 158 ± 7mm and 188 ± 7mm for Chinese people, which shows that typical deviations are in the order of a few percent and the assumption of a constant head size is feasible. Thus, the head width and height, and their respective halves x_m, y_m, are constant for each observation:

$x_m, y_m = const.$ Inserting half the width x_m into the u-coordinate part of equation (4.7) yields

$$u_m = -\frac{g}{sz_m} x_m + o_x \tag{4.8}$$

and consequently

$$\frac{g}{sz_m} = -\frac{u_m - o_x}{x_m} = const \tag{4.9}$$

because u_m, o_x (see observation 1) and x_m are constant.

The same argumentation holds for using the y- and v-coordinates respectively. A constant value for $\frac{g}{sz_m}$ means that the virtual sensor also changes and fits to the size of the light rays of the face boundary, if the distance z_m between the face and the camera varies, which is illustrated in figure 4.6c.

3. **The large capturing distance** in surveillance setups leads to the depth of the face being negligible in comparison to the distance between camera and head: $|z_h - z_m| \ll z_h$ and thus $z_h \approx z_m$ for any z_h referring to a point on the head.

To prove the claim that $(u,v,\alpha,\beta,\gamma)^T$ uniquely identifies the face position $\boldsymbol{\xi}$, it has to be shown that for identical given head pose and image coordinates $(u,v,\alpha,\beta,\gamma)^T = (\widehat{u},\widehat{v},\widehat{\alpha},\widehat{\beta},\widehat{\gamma})^T$, the respective face positions $\boldsymbol{\xi} = (X,Y,Z)^T$ and $\widehat{\boldsymbol{\xi}} = (\widehat{X},\widehat{Y},\widehat{Z})^T$ are identical. First, as an intermediate step, the following derivation shows the equality of camera coordinates in x- and y-direction in this case:

$$\begin{pmatrix} x \\ y \end{pmatrix} = -\frac{sz}{g} \cdot \begin{pmatrix} u - o_x \\ v - o_y \end{pmatrix} \tag{4.10}$$

$$\approx -\frac{sz_m}{g} \cdot \begin{pmatrix} u - o_x \\ v - o_y \end{pmatrix} \tag{4.11}$$

$$= -\frac{\widehat{s}\widehat{z}_m}{\widehat{g}} \cdot \begin{pmatrix} \widehat{u} - \widehat{o}_x \\ \widehat{v} - \widehat{o}_y \end{pmatrix} \tag{4.12}$$

$$\approx -\frac{\widehat{s}\widehat{z}}{\widehat{g}} \cdot \begin{pmatrix} \widehat{u} - \widehat{o}_x \\ \widehat{v} - \widehat{o}_y \end{pmatrix} = \begin{pmatrix} \widehat{x} \\ \widehat{y} \end{pmatrix}. \tag{4.13}$$

Equations (4.11) and (4.13) hold under the approximation in observation 3 with $z \approx z_m$. Then, the constant factor from equation (4.9) leads to (4.12).

Altogether starting from $\boldsymbol{\xi}$, the argumentation is

$$\boldsymbol{\xi} = \begin{pmatrix} X \\ Y \\ Z \end{pmatrix} = R^{-1} \begin{pmatrix} x \\ y \\ z \end{pmatrix} - \boldsymbol{t} \tag{4.14}$$

$$= R^{-1} \begin{pmatrix} x \\ y \\ z_m \end{pmatrix} - \begin{pmatrix} 0 \\ 0 \\ z_m \end{pmatrix} \tag{4.15}$$

$$= R^{-1} \begin{pmatrix} \widehat{x} \\ \widehat{y} \\ \widehat{z} \end{pmatrix} - \widehat{\boldsymbol{t}} = \begin{pmatrix} \widehat{X} \\ \widehat{Y} \\ \widehat{Z} \end{pmatrix} = \widehat{\boldsymbol{\xi}} \tag{4.16}$$

with observations 1 and 3 leading to (4.15), and together with the intermediate derivations (4.10)-(4.13) to (4.16).

Because the image position and the head pose uniquely encode the measurement conditions, an encoding vector $\boldsymbol{e}$ holding all information is

$$\boldsymbol{e} = \begin{pmatrix} u \\ v \\ \alpha \\ \beta \\ \gamma \end{pmatrix}. \tag{4.17}$$

For a given feature vector, in this case an LBP histogram $\boldsymbol{h}$ that describes the face under the encoded conditions $\boldsymbol{e}$, the encoded feature is

$$\boldsymbol{h}_e = \begin{pmatrix} \boldsymbol{h} \\ J\boldsymbol{e} \end{pmatrix} \tag{4.18}$$

where J is a diagonal weight matrix. Note that this strategy is transferable to any other local features besides LBP, such as SIFT, LDP, or MCT. Altogether, the feature encoding provides a method to discriminate features by their measurement conditions even if they are collected in an unstructured way.

4.1.4 LBP Descriptor Summary

The proposed LBP descriptor offers an invariance to monotonic illumination changes by design. A robustness to LR applications is incorporated by the proposed histogram fusion strategy. In addition, it is unaffected by overfitting effects, because it is a completely unsupervised method, and the local character of the feature extraction allows the application of according sequence descriptors. The potential shortcomings of this strategy include that no robustness to further challenges in low-quality data is guaranteed. Also, depending on the chosen meta-parameters, the descriptor size can easily exceed 1000 dimensions. Finally, the descriptor is rather general and can conceptually only be weakly adapted to the face domain. This means, the prior information that the descriptor is extracted from a face image instead of anything else might be used more efficiently.

4.2 Supervised: Convolutional Neural Network

Recent approaches to represent HR face images are often based on CNNs. The proposed supervised strategy follows this concept as well and includes improvements to successfully address the LR target scenario. As argued before in section 3.4, fine-tuning on pre-trained networks is impossible for LR applications which is why the networks have to be trained from scratch [Her16c]. This raises the question which of the recent state-of-the-art CNN architectures are best suitable for the LR task [Her17]. The three currently most distinctive and widespread architecture types are the inception architecure [Sze15a, Sze15b], the residual architecture [He15a, He16] and the rather classically designed VGG architecture [Sim15], which is quite similar to the well known AlexNet [Kri12]. Because it is unclear which architecture suites best, all three will be adapted and explored for the LR face recognition scenario.

For the ease of presentation in this section, the input face image size is assumed to be fixed at 32×32 pixels. Further low-resolution face sizes ranging from 8×8 to 40×40 pixels will be addressed in the evaluation in chapter 6.

The result of this section will be a trained network $\mathcal{C}$ which projects face images $\boldsymbol{u}$ to face image descriptors $\mathcal{V} = \boldsymbol{v} = \mathcal{C}(\boldsymbol{u})$. The descriptor vectors $\boldsymbol{v} \in \mathbb{R}^d$ will be of low dimension d to allow fast processing in large-scale retrieval applications. The network $\mathcal{C}$ is learned in a supervised manner from face images labeled with the respective person identity.

4.2.1 Network Architecture

The main issue when adapting the different HR architectures to LR scenarios are the downsampling layers which are usually implemented as pooling layers. They group spatial information by propagating the average or maximum of a $P \times P$ region. The common choice of using a stride of 2, i.e., to evaluate the receptive field only at every second position, results in a downsampling by a factor of two. If some spatial information should be kept in the deepest feature maps, a maximum of 4 pooling layers is acceptable for 32×32 pixel input size and the most favorable choice of $P = 2$. The 5th pooling layer would condense the remaining 2×2 feature map into a 1×1 feature map and destroy the respective spatial information.

This conflicts with one general rule of thumb for designing CNNs stating that deeper networks are preferred over wider networks. When depth is limited by the maximum number of possible downsampling steps, it will be necessary to compromise by using wider networks than for HR applications.

Because it is unclear beforehand which compromise will be best, as many meta-parameters of the network as feasible will be systematically optimized. This includes the number of filters per convolutional layer (influenced by G), the pooling region size ($P \times P$) and the number of fully connected neurons (influenced by H). Stride and padding are chosen in a way that as little data as possible will be lost in the process. In addition, the structure of the network is optimized for each architecture type as stated in the respective section. Due to the highly variable network architecture, the number of network parameters varies significantly and lies between 0.8M and 159M for the evaluated settings on 32×32 pixels input.

Classical Architecture

The classical philosophy became popular with the famous AlexNet [Kri12] and was extended with minor adaptations in the VGG Face network [Par15]. Conceptually, the beginning of a network consists of alternating convolutional and pooling layers, as illustrated in figure 4.7a. After these layers, a set of fully connected layers is appended to classify the resulting feature maps of the first layers. As motivated by the authors of the VGG network [Sim15], in this architecture, consecutive convolutional layers can be understood as a replacement of a single convolutional layer with a larger filter size. This means, for example, that two 3×3 convolutional layers are a replacement for one 5×5 convolutional layer. Following this motivation, the number of layers in such a network has to remain limited for LR applications because small filter sizes are required to represent the small content size in the LR image. Large filter sizes in the shape of many consecutive convolutional layers are unnecessary or even counterproductive.

Design choices for this architecture type include the number of convolutional, pooling and fully connected layers. To ease optimization, the basic structure of the network starts with a 3×3 convolutional layer and continues with a varying number N_g of groups each consisting of N_c 3×3 convolutional layers and one pooling layer at the end. After the convolutional groups, a varying number N_f of fully connected layers is added.

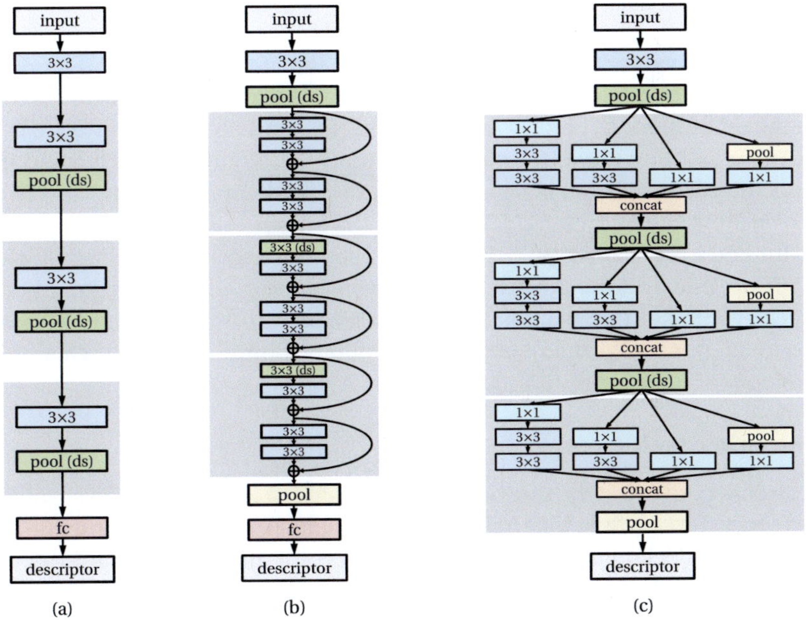

Figure 4.7: Adapted LR networks for different architecture types: classical (a), residual (b) and inception (c). Green background denotes downsampling layers (ds).

Residual Architecture

The main difference to the classical architecture is an identity bypass of two convolutional layers (figure 4.7b). The benefit according to He et al. [He15a] is the better trainability for very deep networks. Instead of learning a direct function mapping of the input $\boldsymbol{x}$ to the output $f(\boldsymbol{x})$ where f represents the learned function, this strategy has to learn only an offset or residual $f(\boldsymbol{x})$ to the identity, leading to the output $f(\boldsymbol{x}) + \boldsymbol{x}$. The authors argue that the identity mapping serves as preconditioning for network training and show experimentally that the offsets are small compared with learning f directly. Using this trick, this architecture type currently allows the deepest networks with up to 1000 layers in certain applications [He16]. Because the potentially lower number of layers in the scope of this thesis reduces training time, the regular full-sized residual blocks instead of the reduced bottleneck ones are employed. This avoids the in this architecture unnecessary 1×1 convolutional layers which reduce the data dimension in the reduced bottleneck blocks. A specialty of the residual architecture are the missing pooling layers for downsampling. This is instead performed by specific convolutional layers, which have a stride of 2, resulting also in a downsampling by factor 2. Once again, the amount of these special layers is limited in LR scenarios. Calling a fixed set of consecutive residual blocks a group, one of these downsampling layers is inserted at the beginning of each group. Key design choices for this architecture include the number of residual groups N_g, their sizes in terms of block number N_b, as well as the number of trailing fully connected layers N_f.

Inception Architecture

The core concept of the inception architecture is a kind of meta layer called an inception module [Sze15a, Sze15b] depicted in figure 4.7c. It includes several parallel data processing paths which are motivated by multi-scale processing. Efficient usage of computing resources is implemented by 1×1 convolutional layers which reduce data dimension. This is similar to the reduced bottleneck blocks in the residual architecture. But in contrast, they have to be included in the inception architecture at all times to limit parameters in the highly parallel inception module. The key design choice is the number of inception modules N_g and trailing fully connected layers N_f. Filter numbers within an inception module are fixed to a ratio of 1:4:2:1 for the double 3×3, single 3×3, 1×1 and pooling path, respectively. The filter number ratio between 1×1 and consecutive 3×3 layers is 1:2. Following the same argumentation about filter sizes as for the classical architecture, a pooling layer follows after each inception module to avoid overly large filter sizes. The combination of inception module and pooling layer is called a group.

Common Design Choices

As illustrated in the examples in figure 4.7, the basic structure of each network begins with a 3×3 convolutional layer after the input, followed by a pooling layer in case of residual and inception architectures. Afterwards, a modifiable number N_g of layer groups of the respective architecture kind is added. The number of convolutional filters G is doubled after each group in the network. In all cases, downsampling is performed between layer groups. The networks end with a varying number of fully connected layers N_f in front of the output layer which holds the face image descriptor. Batch normalization [Iof15] and the ReLU activation function [Kri12] are applied throughout the networks after each convolutional and fully connected layer.

4.2.2 Data Augmentation

Even though the self-collected IOSB-SURV dataset has a considerable size, it is infeasible to train a neural network with it. As mentioned before, it is also economically unreasonable to create a sufficiently large surveillance training dataset because of the required manual labeling as no assisting metadata and image tags are available for such data. Thus, training with existing large high-quality face datasets is required. The problem consists in the domain gap between these datasets and the surveillance domain, because they are mainly automatically collected high-quality celebrity (e.g., CASIA WebFace [Yi14], Celebrity-1000 [Liu14], FaceScrub [Ng14], MS-Celeb-1M (MS1M) [Guo16], MSRA-CFW [Zha12a], TVC, YTF [Wol11], VGG [Par15]) or personal (MegaFace [Nec16]) face images from the web.

Two strategies are proposed for target domain adaptation [Her16b]. First, in addition to public datasets, the self-collected TVC face video dataset is added. Although collected from professional TV footage, this video data is much closer to the target domain than public single image datasets. It has similar image quality as the YTF or Celebrity-1000 dataset, but is significantly larger than the former and has less label errors and a higher diversity than the latter. Second, image transformations are proposed that adjust the public high-quality datasets to be similar to the low-quality target domain

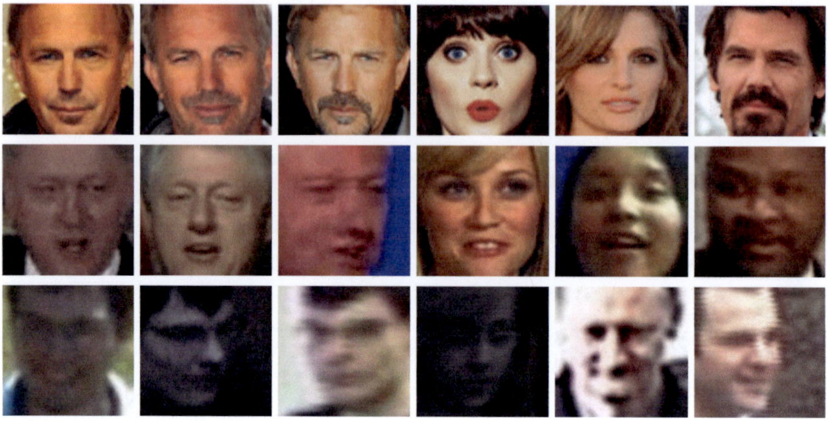

Figure 4.8: Qualitative comparison of face images from FaceScrub (top), YTF (center) and IOSB-SURV (bottom). It can be seen that video data (YTF and IOSB-SURV) has less quality than single image, mugshot-like data (FaceScrub). However, professional video recordings (YTF) show still better quality than surveillance data (IOSB-SURV).

with respect to the image quality properties. Obviously, the first stage is required to be an adjustment to the chosen target resolution which will be between 8×8 and 40×40 pixels face size.

The next significant domain difference is blur. The sharpness level s of IOSB-SURV and downsampled versions of FaceScrub and YTF is compared by the maximum response of a Laplacian filter $\mathcal{L}$. High responses of the Laplacian filter denote sharp edges which are typical for unblurred images. Thus, filter responses can be understood as sharpness level

$$s = \max \mathcal{L}(\boldsymbol{u}) \,. \tag{4.19}$$

Downsampled FaceScrub images at 32×32 pixels show an average sharpness level of $s = 0.534$ and YTF images of $s = 0.352$, compared with $s = 0.304$ for IOSB-SURV face images. This correlates well with the subjective image quality, as illustrated in figure 4.8. According to further tests, the difference corresponds on average to blurring the FaceScrub images with a Gaussian kernel with a standard deviation of $\sigma = 0.6$ or a motion kernel of 5 pixels length ($\sigma = 0.4$ and 1.5 pixels for YTF). A horizontal motion kernel is an image filter created by normalizing an odd-sized square matrix with 1 on the center row and 0 elsewhere. Rotated motion kernels can be generated by rotating this base kernel by image interpolation rules. Note that blur in surveillance data is usually motion blur caused by object movement and exposure time of the camera. The image formation process involves some further effects besides motion blur and scale effects including noisy images caused by sensor noise as well as artifacts caused by compression requirements to transmit the data.

All in all, this leads to seven different augmentation strategies, as illustrated in figure 4.9. The first geometric three are inspired by literature [Par15, McL15]: flipping, cropping, rotation. The last four by the domain requirements: motion blur, noise, compression and rescaling. Because rescaling already covers isotropic blur by its anti-aliasing filtering, no dedicated isotropic blur augmentation is added. Low-quality challenges listed in section 1.2 with no according domain augmentation strategy are either already covered adequately by the training data diversity (head poses, occlusions), very rare (lens distortions) or too difficult to simulate with sufficient realism (bad illumination).

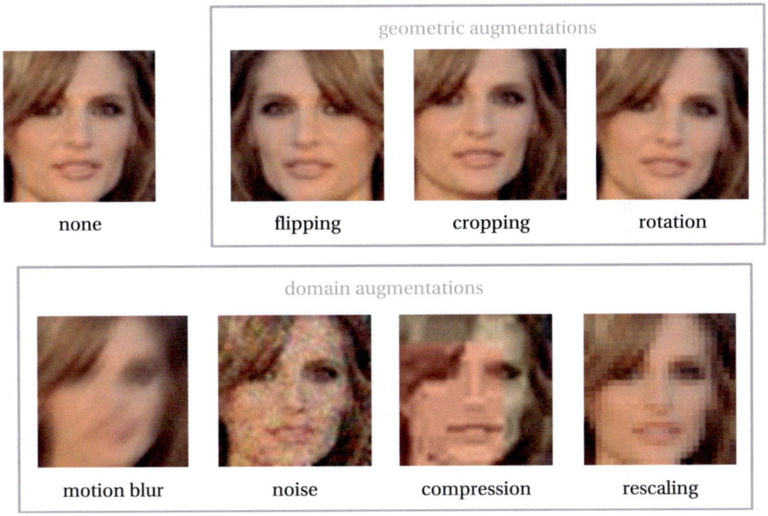

Figure 4.9: Training data augmentation strategies.

For a training sample, each augmentation is applied at runtime with a certain predefined probability and a bounded random effectiveness presented in detail by table 4.2 which reflects the empirical frequency and intensity of each effect in the target domain. With this strategy, it is possible that a sample is augmented simultaneously by more than one effect and that it is augmented differently in different training epochs.

Table 4.2: Training data augmentation strategies with their application probabilities and intensity for each training sample. Unless normal distribution $\mathcal{N}$ is denoted, uniform distribution is applied. Intensity parameters assume [0,1] pixel value range. c denotes the number of activated domain augmentations when combining several augmentations strategies.

augmentation	probability	intensity
crop	$\frac{4}{5}$	up to $\frac{1}{16}$ face size
flip	$\frac{1}{2}$	
rotation	$\frac{1}{2}$	$\mathcal{N}(0,2)$ degrees
motion blur	$\frac{1}{2c}$	length up to $\frac{1}{6}$ face size, random direction
noise	$\frac{1}{10c}$	up to $\mathcal{N}(0,0.01)$
compression	$\frac{1}{10c}$	jpeg quality down to 6
rescale	$\frac{1}{10c}$	up to factor 1.4

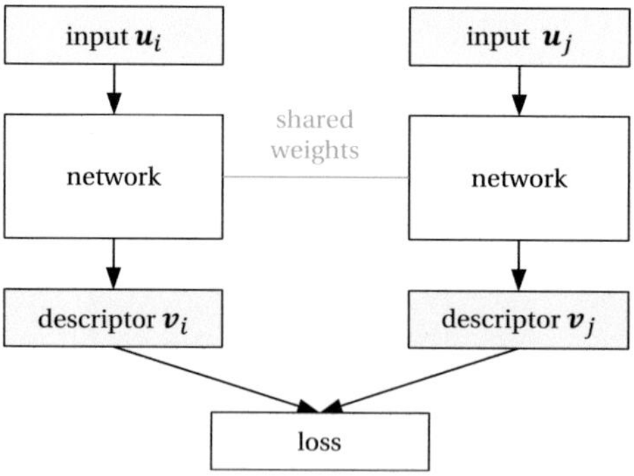

Figure 4.10: Siamese network training concept.

4.2.3 Loss Function

Similar to [Cho05] and [Sch15b], the network is understood as a function $\mathcal{C}$ that maps the input face image $\boldsymbol{u}$ to a target space that is discriminative for face matching: $\mathcal{C}(\boldsymbol{u}) = \boldsymbol{v}$. This leads to a Siamese training setup [Bro94] having the three previously in section 3.4 indicated advantages compared with a conventional softmax classification strategy. First, the descriptor dimension can be chosen arbitrarily and much smaller. Second, the matching distance is directly modeled. And third, it allows an easy combination of training datasets.

Furthermore, a current neurobiological study [Cha17] indicates that the primate brain represents faces in a similar manner with a limited set of brain cells spanning a metric face space. This contradicts the concept of one dedicated cell for each face identity which would be analogue to the softmax classification strategy in CNN terminology where one neuron is present for each face identity.

The Siamese structure illustrated in figure 4.10 can be understood as a network that consists of two branches, each one processing one face image of a pair. Each branch has the same network structure as previously defined.

The loss function minimizes the Euclidean distance between face image descriptors $\boldsymbol{v}$ for positive face pairs (same identity) while maximizing the distance for negative pairs (different identity). For application after training, only one branch of the two identical branches is kept and it projects a face image $\boldsymbol{u}$ into the target descriptor space where comparison to further face image descriptors is quickly possible by Euclidean distance. As dimension of the target face image descriptor space, a small size of $d = 128$ has repeatedly proven to be an appropriate choice [Sch15b, Her16c, Sim13, Par14]. In addition, the primate brain appears to employ around 200 cells to encode faces [Cha17], supporting this order of the dimension d. The proposed loss function L is a max-margin hinge loss formulation

$$L_{\text{max-margin}} = \sum_{i,j} \max\left(0, 1 - y_{ij} \cdot \left(\eta - \mathcal{D}_e^2(\boldsymbol{v}_i, \boldsymbol{v}_j)\right)\right), \tag{4.20}$$

similar to [Sim13], where $\boldsymbol{v}_i$ and $\boldsymbol{v}_j$ denote the face image descriptors, η the decision boundary, $\mathcal{D}_e^2$ the squared Euclidean distance and $y_{ij} = \{-1, 1\}$ the indicator variable where $y_{ij} = 1$ if and only if $\boldsymbol{v}_i$ and $\boldsymbol{v}_j$ show the same identity. This is the hinge loss formulation for requesting the squared Euclidean distance $\mathcal{D}_e^2(\boldsymbol{v}_i,\boldsymbol{v}_j) = ||\boldsymbol{v}_i - \boldsymbol{v}_j||_2^2$ to be discriminative with respect to face matching in a general max-margin sense

$$\mathcal{D}_e^2(\boldsymbol{v}_i,\boldsymbol{v}_j)\begin{cases} \leq \eta - 1 & \text{if } y_{ij} = 1 \\ \geq \eta + 1 & \text{if } y_{ij} = -1 \end{cases} . \tag{4.21}$$

Thus, for face image pairs with matching identities, i.e. $y_{ij} = 1$, the network should project them onto nearby descriptors in the target space which have a squared Euclidean distance below a decision boundary η minus a margin. For non-matching pairs, i.e. $y_{ij} = -1$, the network should project the images onto distant descriptors outside η and the margin. The decision boundary η is considered a trainable parameter of the loss and is learned by back-propagation.

The benefit of the max-margin loss function compared with the common contrastive loss [Had06]

$$L_{\text{contrastive}} = \frac{1}{2}\sum_{i,j}\left(\left(1 + y_{ij}\right)\mathcal{D}_e^2(\boldsymbol{v}_i,\boldsymbol{v}_j) + \left(1 - y_{ij}\right)\cdot\max\left(0,\eta - \mathcal{D}_e^2(\boldsymbol{v}_i,\boldsymbol{v}_j)\right)\right) \tag{4.22}$$

for Siamese setups is that it prevents pushing the distance of a correctly classified positive pair towards 0 if classification is easy, i.e., it lies far from the decision border, as illustrated in figure 4.11. This can avoid overfitting effects. It is more similar in its character to the triplet loss [Sch15b]

$$L_{\text{triplet}} = \sum_i \max\left(0,\mathcal{D}_e^2(\boldsymbol{v}_i^a,\boldsymbol{v}_i^p) - \mathcal{D}_e^2(\boldsymbol{v}_i^a,\boldsymbol{v}_i^n) + \eta\right), \tag{4.23}$$

but reduces complexity by separating positive and negative pairs. The triplet loss is based on anchor samples $\boldsymbol{v}^a$ having the same identity as a positive $\boldsymbol{v}^p$ but a different one as a negative $\boldsymbol{v}^n$ sample.

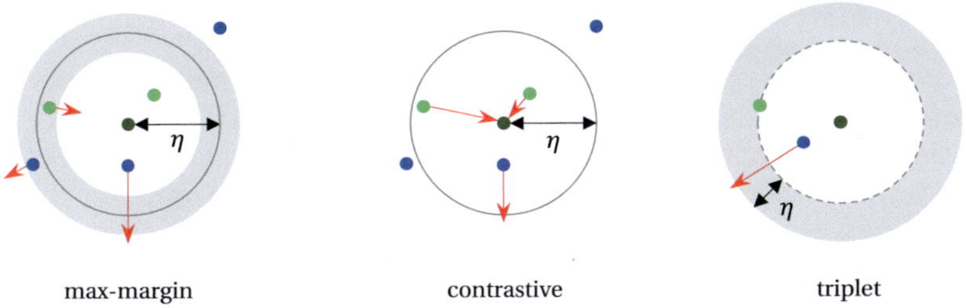

Figure 4.11: Comparative illustration of different loss concepts. Shows the anchor sample (dark green) and the training behavior (red) of samples with the same (light green) or different (blue) identity.

4.2.4 Training Process

The networks are trained by stochastic gradient descent with momentum and weight decay (section 2.3). This requires an appropriate selection of the training batches $\mathcal{B}$. For Siamese networks, a batch consists of n pairs of input face images $(\boldsymbol{u}_1,\boldsymbol{u}_2)$ and n indicator variables y_{12} denoting for each pair if both images show the same identity or not. This allows to easily mix pairs from different datasets within one batch, because the indicator variable is unaffected by further datasets. Note that this is different to a classification setup, where class labels have to be consistent across merged datasets, which is difficult to achieve for face datasets. Celebrity names in public datasets are sometimes spelled differently in different datasets which is especially true for romanized names where different conversions of the original spelling might exist. This makes the necessary identity merge prone to errors. Generating mixed pairs with face images from different datasets involves the same problem which is why no such pairs are created.

Each batch $\mathcal{B}$ is constructed dynamically while training the network with an equal number of positive and negative pairs. The number of pairs from each dataset within a batch is chosen based on dataset size and fixed throughout the training. Augmentations are performed separately for each image in the batch to generate random cross-domain pairs and also different effects within one batch. So if the same pair is included again in a later training batch, the augmentation strategy ensures that it is highly unlikely to look the same as before which increases training set diversity.

4.2.5 CNN Descriptor Summary

Altogether, the supervised strategy leverages the vast amount of externally available face data to learn a compact CNN-based face image descriptor which is highly optimized for the face recognition task. Robustness to challenges in low-quality data is learned from the data by the proposed domain augmentation strategies together with the LR adaptations of the network. Compared with the unsupervised strategy, there are no inherently guaranteed invariances and if the training data and strategy is chosen poorly, overfitting might occur.

5 Face Sequence Representation

The previous chapter explained how each frame $\boldsymbol{u}_i$ in a face track T is described by a face image descriptor $\mathcal{V}_i$. In the next step for fast track matching, a unified representation for the descriptor set $\mathcal{C}(T) = (\mathcal{V}_1, \dots, \mathcal{V}_n)$ of one face track is required: $\mathcal{C}(T) \mapsto \mathcal{W}$. An inverted index solution is proposed in combination with the unsupervised LBP face image descriptor [Her15b] and a center-based strategy for the supervised CNN face image descriptor [Her16c].

5.1 Requirements and Baselines

The track descriptor $\mathcal{W}$ should fulfill several specific requirements to be of practical use:

- independence of track length n,
- compactness,
- fast comparability and
- high recognition performance.

There are only few approaches in literature which satisfy all of these requirements in principle. The most notable one is the Mutual Subspace Method (MSM) [Fuk05] because it offers an excellent trade-off between the requirements. The VF^2 Fisher-Vector faces descriptor [Par14] offers an even more compact representation, but lacks generalization capabilities due to significant domain overfitting. Further common baseline approaches fail at least one requirement:

- Best-shot selection, meaning to select the best descriptor $\mathcal{W} = \mathcal{V}_b$ of the sequence according to some quality criterion, has usually a low matching performance.
- Pair-wise comparison of all or a selected set of image descriptors $\mathcal{V}$ is slow and $\mathcal{W} = \{\mathcal{V}_1, \ldots, \mathcal{V}_k\}$ would be non-compact and usually dependent of the track length.

More complex sequence representations as common for manifold-based and probabilistic descriptors are computationally infeasible for large-scale processing.

5.2 Bag-of-Words and Inverted Index for Local Descriptors

An efficient solution for large-scale visual database retrieval tasks is the accumulative bag-of-words descriptor combined with an inverted index search strategy [Siv03]. One key concept is to represent the image content by local features making a combination with the proposed unsupervised LBP features feasible.

5.2.1 Collecting Features Across Frames

Instead of using descriptors based on whole frames as common for conventional sequence descriptors, a different strategy is applied, as illustrated in figure 5.1 [Her15b]. For comparison, the conventional frame based method is shown at the top, which uses a face descriptor $\mathcal{V}_j$ for each frame j, constructed by the concatenation of several local feature vectors $\boldsymbol{h}_{ij}$, where i denotes the feature location. The final track descriptor $\mathcal{W}$ is derived from the sequence $(\mathcal{V}_1, \ldots, \mathcal{V}_n)$ of all n frame descriptors. The feature based track description $\mathcal{W}'$ is shown at the bottom. In this case, the face descriptor $\mathcal{V}'_j$ is only a mathematical utility, but has no meaning by itself. Basically, all local features $\boldsymbol{h}_{ij}$ are combined into one feature set, which serves as track descriptor $\mathcal{W}'$. There are three advantages of this method:

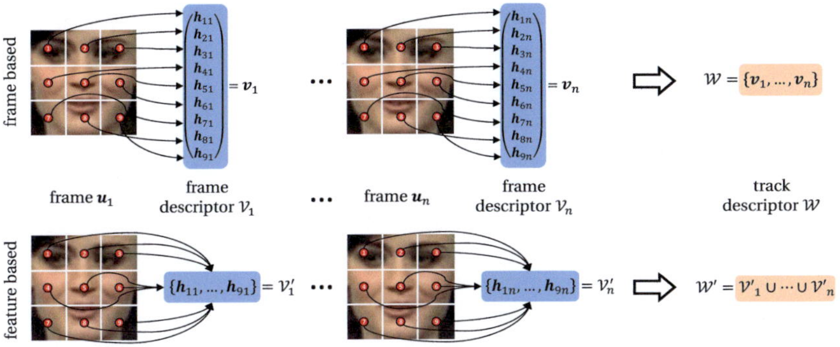

Figure 5.1: Illustration of the conventional frame based track description method (top) and the applied feature set based one (bottom). Local features are denoted by $\boldsymbol{h}_{ij}$.

1. The dimension $d' = q$ of the vectors in $\mathcal{W}'$ is lower than that of the vectors in $\mathcal{W}$, because $\mathcal{W}'$ consists of the smaller feature vectors $\boldsymbol{h}_{ij}$ instead of frame descriptors $\mathcal{V}$. Thus, further processing might be performed faster, because generally all matching approaches scale at least linearly with d'.
2. This representation ignores temporal information. While loosing information is generally a bad idea, it is the opposite in this case, because temporal information includes no clues about a persons identity. For example, the fact that the head rotates in the face track includes no information about who is rotating his or her head.
3. The feature based representation is widely applied in object or image retrieval tasks, which means according approaches can be applied to face retrieval too.

5.2.2 Bag-of-Words and Inverted Index

Generally speaking, a retrieval scenario involves a database of N objects and a query object $\mathcal{Q}$. The task is to find all matching objects to the query object in the database. Basically, the bag-of-words method combined with an inverted index consists of three steps, depicted also in figure 5.2:

1. **Description of objects** with visual words. Each object, in this case each face track T, is described by a set of predefined visual words. Possible visual words are defined by a codebook (dictionary) which is constructed by clustering all the object features of the database in K

classes and using the cluster centers $\mu_1,\ldots,\mu_K$ as visual words. In this way, the codebook consists of domain specific visual words. Note that the clustering is an unsupervised method which requires no external or additional data besides the actual database. Thus, no overfitting to out-of-domain data can occur. Note that in-domain overfitting of the codebook is still possible, e.g.by choosing an overly large number of clusters K. For each object, the feature set $\mathcal{W}'$ from the previous section is computed and the matching words are found by assigning each feature to the nearest visual word. The set of present words, usually referred to as the *bag-of-words*, represents the object. The bag-of-words vector $\boldsymbol{\varphi} \in \mathbb{R}^K_{\geq 0}$ consists of the occurrence frequencies ω_i of each visual word μ_i in the represented object.

2. **Building an inverted index** for the whole database of objects. To avoid a linear search for the best matches in the database based on the high-dimensional but sparse bag-of-words vectors $\boldsymbol{\varphi}$, an inverted index is applied. This means an index I with all visual words from the codebook is constructed and for each visual word, a list of all database objects O_j including this visual word is maintained: $I: \mu_i \mapsto \{O_j \mid \mu_i \text{ is part of } O_j\}$.
3. **Database query by indexed search** for the query visual words. Performing a search for the query object $\mathcal{Q}$ first requires to extract its visual words. Then, for each visual word of the query object, the matching database objects are looked up in the index. Finally, accumulating the number of hits for the matching database objects results in a ranking. In large scale applications it is common that a significant part of the database objects has no hits at all.

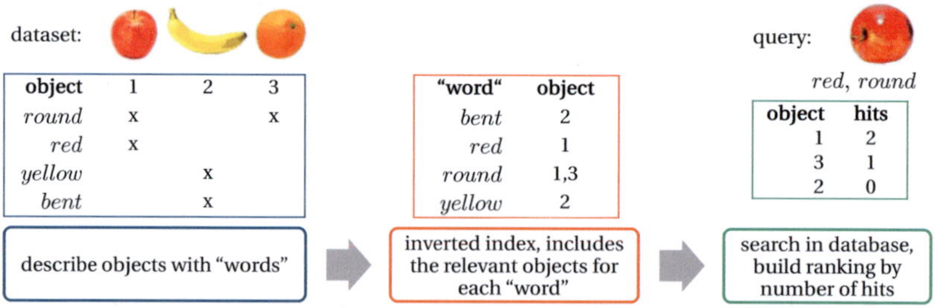

Figure 5.2: Illustration of the inverted index approach with a basic example using images of fruit instead of face tracks and regular words instead of visual ones.

5.2.3 Improved Inverted Index

Using the inverted index strategy without adaptation has a serious drawback. Because all visual features are put together into a single feature set, their location in the face is lost. While this behavior is usually desired in image retrieval applications, because it guarantees invariance to rotation, scaling and shifting, it is counterproductive in face retrieval and leads to low retrieval results [Wu11]. Face detections are always aligned, thus they have a known and fixed rotation, scale and are shifted equally. In this way, the feature location is meaningful in contradiction to general image retrieval and it promises to improve the results. Because the nose is always in the middle, eyes at the top, mouth at the bottom and so on, comparing features from different locations is unnecessary. It has no meaning if the nose of one person shows the same feature as the eye of another one.

Two solutions to address this problem exist:

1. Implicit location involvement by augmenting the local features with the respective image coordinates, as presented in section 4.1.3, separates the visual words according to feature locations in the face on clustering. This is caused by the location distance becoming part of the descriptor distance $\mathcal{D}(\boldsymbol{h}_{e,1}, \boldsymbol{h}_{e,2})$ which is applied for clustering. Depending on the weight matrix J, this is more of a soft assignment of the local features to one another based on location.
2. Explicit location exploitation by constructing separate inverted indices I_j [Her15b]. Instead of using one single inverted index I for all features, separate local indices I_j, as shown at the bottom of figure 5.3, are proposed. Each feature location in the fixed grid is handled individually and results are combined at the end by accumulating the hit counts from the different index searches. This strategy leads to a hard assignment of features to locations where no local features from different location will be compared to each other.

Because the feature variety within a local region is smaller than across the whole face image, the local indices can be chosen smaller in the second case. Targeting the same memory complexity, each of the N local indices has to be of size $\frac{K}{N}$. The advantages compared with the first option are a faster index generation, because constructing N small indices of size $\frac{K}{N}$ over $\frac{F}{N}$ features is faster than constructing one large index of size K over F features. The faster construction becomes obvious in the case of the commonly applied Lloyd algorithm for k-means clustering with an expected complexity of $\mathcal{O}(qKF)$ for q-dimensionsal local features [Kan02]. The construction complexity in the local case then becomes $N \cdot \mathcal{O}(q \cdot \frac{K}{N} \cdot \frac{F}{N}) = \mathcal{O}(\frac{qKF}{N})$. In addition, parallel processing of the local regions offers further practical speedup potential which is also exploitable in the query case.

Altogether, the inverted index strategy satisfies all technical requirements from section 5.1. The bag-of-words vector $\boldsymbol{\varphi}$ accumulates all occurring words, making it independent of track length and the inverted index creates a compact representation which allows fast face search.

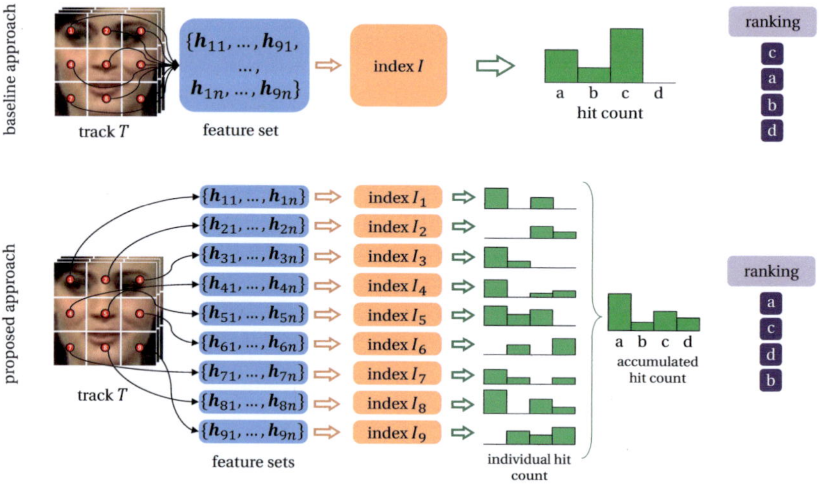

Figure 5.3: Comparison of the baseline (top) and the proposed (bottom) inverted index strategy. The illustration shows a query process for a small sample database whose face tracks are called a, b, c and d.

5.3 Center-Based Representation for CNN Descriptors

The supervised CNN-based image descriptors are holistic thus the same approach as for the local LBP descriptors is infeasible. Instead, a track descriptor $\mathcal{W}$ based on centers in the face image descriptor space is proposed and it will be shown that it satisfies all of the requirements. It is motivated by considerations about the CNN and its target space properties.

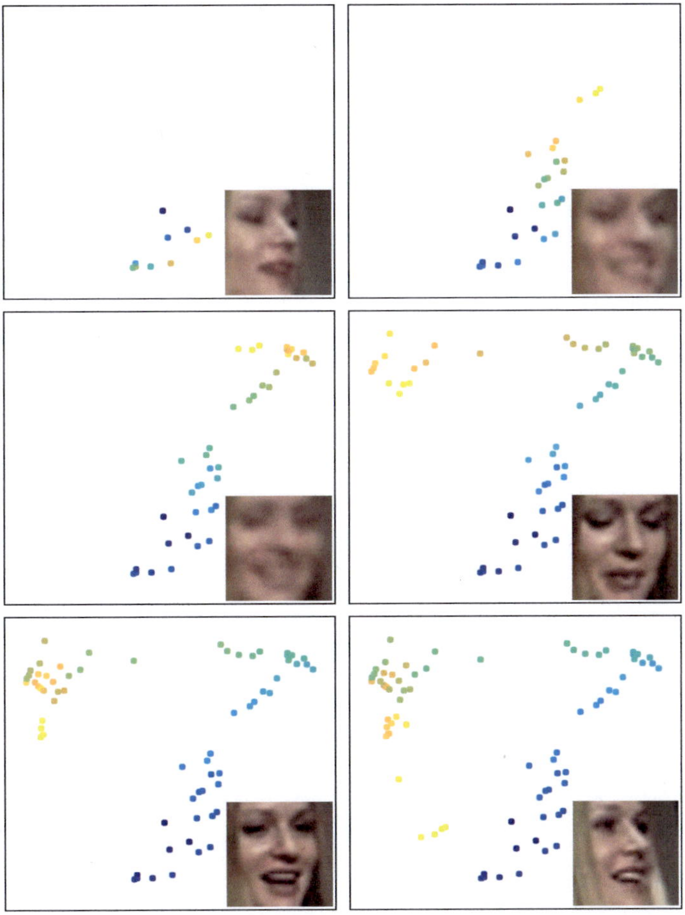

Figure 5.4: Projection of CNN face image descriptors from a sample face sequence in a 2D space via PCA. Illustrated at different time steps with 10, 25, 40, 55, 70 and all (79) frames. Latest descriptors are indicated in yellowish colors and the face corresponding to the most recently added descriptor is indicated in the respective lower right corner. It can be observed that both principal axes of the descriptor space mainly correspond to two visible effects in this case: head rotation (vertical) and blur (horizontal).

5.3.1 The Local Mean Method

Initially, the proposed center-based sequence descriptor is presented intuitively following a few observations. Then, the next section will motivate it more formally. Observing the distribution of the face image descriptors $\boldsymbol{v}$ in the target space in figure 5.4 indicates that a noise resistant representation of the descriptor set is required [Her16c]. Local means $\mathcal{W} = \{\boldsymbol{m}_1, \ldots, \boldsymbol{m}_\kappa\}$, determined by k-means clustering of the image descriptor vectors $\boldsymbol{v}$, are proposed to address this and to reduce the amount of data (figure 5.5). In contradiction to more common exemplar based representations, such as selecting key faces [Zha08a] or applying the Ramer-Douglas-Peucker algorithm to select good exemplars, the proposed strategy includes an averaging effect which reduces the given noise.

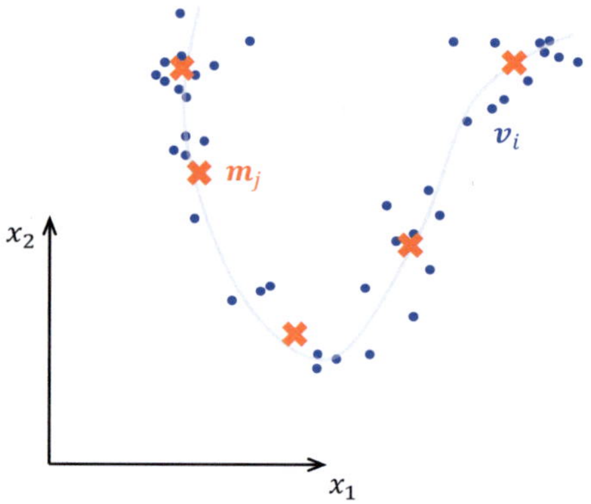

Figure 5.5: Visualization of the proposed center-based sequence descriptor concept.

The descriptor distance $\mathcal{D}(\mathcal{W}_1, \mathcal{W}_2)$ is computed by the pair-wise minimum distance of the local means:

$$\mathcal{D}(\mathcal{W}_1, \mathcal{W}_2) = \min_{\boldsymbol{m}_1 \in \mathcal{W}_1, \boldsymbol{m}_2 \in \mathcal{W}_2} \|\boldsymbol{m}_1 - \boldsymbol{m}_2\|_2 . \tag{5.1}$$

This Local Mean Method (LMM) satisfies the requirements from section 5.1. First, it can be shown experimentally that a compact representation with a small number κ of local patches is sufficient to achieve competitive performance (see figure 6.8) which, second, leads to a low comparison effort.

Third, the LMM descriptor size depends only on κ and the face image descriptor dimension d and is consequently independent of the sequence length. In addition, the method is tolerant to noise affection caused by outliers due to the averaging of the face image descriptors. The next section will provide theoretical insights why a small κ is sufficient and how exactly to choose it.

5.3.2 Motivation by Loss-Function Considerations

The first assumption for the detailed motivation of the proposed sequence descriptor is a well trained CNN. Consequently, the target of the loss function, which was formulated in equation (4.21), is valid for all face image descriptors $\boldsymbol{v}$. Following from this, there exists an upper bound a for the Euclidean distance between face image descriptors from the same person identity C

$$\mathcal{D}_e(\boldsymbol{v}_i,\boldsymbol{v}_j) \leq a = \sqrt{\eta - 1}\,, \quad \text{for } \mathcal{I}(\boldsymbol{v}_i) = \mathcal{I}(\boldsymbol{v}_j) = C \tag{5.2}$$

where $\mathcal{I}(\boldsymbol{v})$ denotes the identity for a given face image descriptor $\boldsymbol{v}$. Let I_C denote the maximum theoretical set of all descriptors with $\mathcal{I}(\boldsymbol{v}) = C$, thus

$$\left(\boldsymbol{v}_i \in I_C \wedge \boldsymbol{v}_j \in I_C\right) \Leftrightarrow \mathcal{D}_e(\boldsymbol{v}_i,\boldsymbol{v}_j) \leq a\,. \tag{5.3}$$

In the next step, the shape of this set I_C will be determined sufficiently to give a motivation on how to design an appropriate sequence descriptor.

Finding the Shape

If equation (5.3) is the only defining restriction for I_C, this will geometrically restrict the space the descriptors of one identity can lie in.

1. It is obvious that the maximum descriptor set I_C of one identity C is convex: if two vectors $\boldsymbol{v}_i,\boldsymbol{v}_j$ lie in I_C then $\mathcal{D}_e(\boldsymbol{v}_i,\boldsymbol{v}_j) \leq a$. Consequently, all vectors on the line segment between $\boldsymbol{v}_i$ and $\boldsymbol{v}_j$ have a distance $\mathcal{D}_e \leq a$ to both ends making the line segment part of I_C which shows convexity.
2. Its limits are bounded by

$$\exists \boldsymbol{m}_C \in \mathbb{R}^d \, \forall \boldsymbol{v} \in I_C : \mathcal{D}_e(\boldsymbol{m}_C,\boldsymbol{v}) \leq \sqrt{\frac{d}{2d+2}} \cdot a\,. \tag{5.4}$$

This states that the maximum descriptor set I_C of one identity lies within a hypersphere with the center $\boldsymbol{m}_C$ and the given radius for dimension d.

The motivation for equation (5.4) is given by the possibilities to distribute a set of points in d-dimensional space while equation (5.3) holds. The shape of the set is non-unique with two extreme cases:

1. The most regular and compact distribution of the descriptors in I_C would be a hypersphere of radius $\frac{a}{2}$ including its hypervolume. This hypersphere is maximal in the sense that no further point can be added to the set without hurting equation (5.3) because opposite points on the hypersphere have a mutual distance of a.
2. The most heterogeneous set distribution is constructed by distributing v points $\boldsymbol{x}_i$ as vertex points of a regular v-simplex with edge length a, because this maximizes the mutual distance between the points while still fulfilling equation (5.3). Of course, all points inside the simplex belong to the set. However, the simplex facets are no bound of the set because there exist points beyond the facets having a distance less than a to the opposing vertex, as illustrated in orange color in figure 5.6 for the 2D case. So the maximized set, where no further points can be added, includes these partial hyperspheres spanned by the vertex points of each facet and the respective opposing vertex point as center. This shape also known as Reuleaux simplex.

In the second case, all descriptors of the identity C are guaranteed to lie within the hyper-circumsphere of the simplex having the radius

$$r = \sqrt{\frac{d}{2d+2}} \cdot a \tag{5.5}$$

for dimension d. At the same time, this is the minimum bounding hypersphere of the set I_C because the simplex vertex points lie on the hypersphere and span it. Note that $r > \frac{a}{2}$ for $d > 1$ which means that the first case of a hypersphere is included in this hyper-circumsphere bound derived from the simplex case. Figure 5.6 illustrates this difference in the 2D case by the green circumscribing circle including the blue disc. Note that there are blue areas outside the orange Reuleaux triangle area but they are still inside the green circumscribing circle around the triangle, which illustrates the validity of the green hyper-circumsphere as minimum bounding hypersphere.

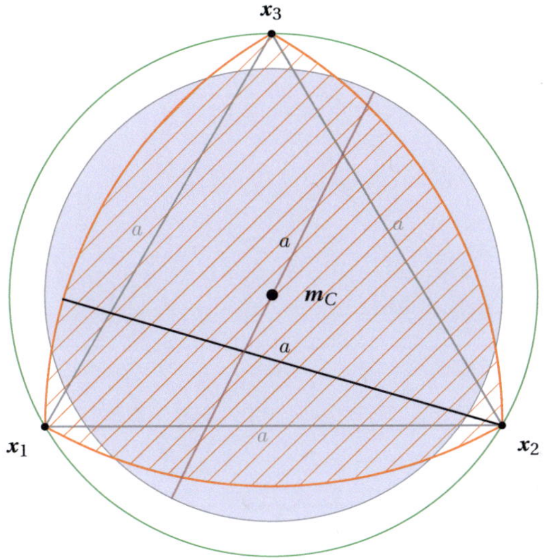

Figure 5.6: Visualization of both extremal cases for the set distribution of I_C for the 2D case: blue sphere area (2D: disk), or orange Reuleaux simplex area based on a regular simplex (2D: equilateral triangle). The simplex circumsphere (2D: circumscribed circle) with radius r is drawn in green.

Exploiting the Shape Properties

Using the center point $\boldsymbol{m}_C$ as descriptor for the identity set I_C maximizes the inter-class distance $\mathcal{D}(C,\widehat{C})$ as it is the point which has maximum distance to the set borders. In particular, the inter-class distance grows bigger than the threshold of $\sqrt{\eta+1}$ enforced by the loss function in equation (4.21). In the most unfavorable case, as illustrated in figure 5.7 for the 2D case, the inter-class distance is

$$\mathcal{D}(C,\widehat{C}) = \mathcal{D}_e(\boldsymbol{m}_C,\boldsymbol{m}_{\widehat{C}}) = 2g + \sqrt{\eta+1} = \tag{5.6}$$

$$= 2\sqrt{\eta-1}\left(1-\sqrt{\frac{d}{2d+2}}\right) + \sqrt{\eta+1} \tag{5.7}$$

with $g = a - r$. So part of the intra-class distance adds to the inter-class distance $\mathcal{D}(C,\widehat{C})$ if enough information to determine $\boldsymbol{m}_C$ is available and a bad selection of $\boldsymbol{m}_C$ is avoided.

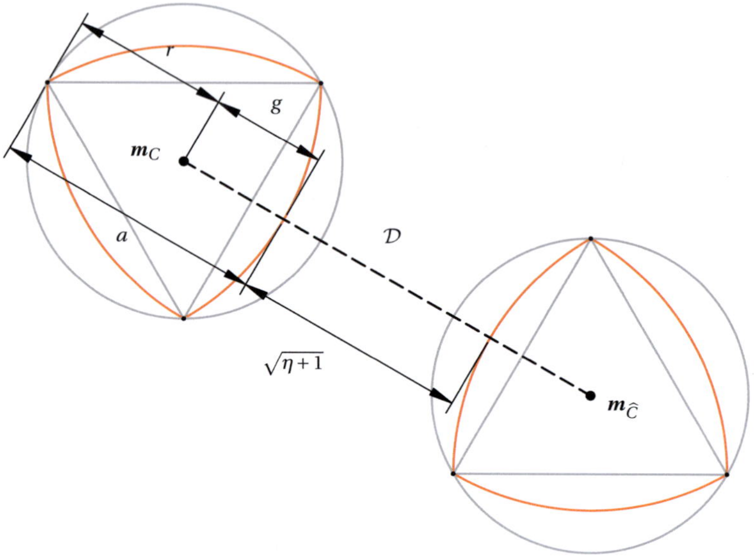

Figure 5.7: Illustration of inter-class distance $\mathcal{D}$.

Necessary Approximations

In practice, the set of available face image descriptors for one identity is limited to one face track. An approximation $\widetilde{\boldsymbol{m}}_C$ for $\boldsymbol{m}_C$ is required which maximizes the distance to neighboring identities $\widehat{C}$, given this incomplete face image descriptor set $\mathcal{C}(T)$ for identity C. Incomplete means that it does not span the whole minimum bounding hypersphere of the identity. Choosing $\widetilde{\boldsymbol{m}}_C = \boldsymbol{v}$ randomly from $\boldsymbol{v} \in I_C$ guarantees only

$$\mathcal{D}_e(\widetilde{\boldsymbol{m}}_C, \widetilde{\boldsymbol{m}}_{\widehat{C}}) \geq \sqrt{\eta+1} \tag{5.8}$$

because of equation (4.21). This distance becomes maximally unfavorable in case $\widetilde{\boldsymbol{m}}_C$ resides at the border of the respective identity set I_C. So choosing the track descriptor $\mathcal{W} = \widetilde{\boldsymbol{m}}_C$ as far off as possible from all borders maximizes the inter-class distance. Potentially good approximation candidates $\widetilde{\boldsymbol{m}}_C$ are consequently

1. the center of the minimum bounding hypersphere,
2. the centroid of the convex hull, or
3. the mean

of the incomplete descriptor set $\mathcal{C}(T)$. In all cases, the resulting $\tilde{\boldsymbol{m}}_{\mathcal{C}}$ would lie inside the convex hull of $\mathcal{C}(T)$. Option 1 and 2 are preferred from a geometric viewpoint yet they are difficult to compute efficiently in high dimensional spaces. In this respect, the mean from option 3 is preferred. Because no algorithms with a feasible computational burden for option 1 and 2 are available for $d = 128$ dimensions and up to several thousand face image descriptors, the chosen track descriptor is

$$\mathcal{W} = \frac{1}{|\mathcal{C}(T)|} \sum_{\boldsymbol{v} \in \mathcal{C}(T)} \boldsymbol{v}\,. \tag{5.9}$$

This is equal to the track descriptor in the previous section for $\kappa = 1$ which allows application of the same track descriptor distance $\mathcal{D}(\mathcal{W}_1, \mathcal{W}_2)$ from equation (5.1).

Note that the argumentation in this section is based on a projection network using the proposed max-margin-based loss. It is also similarly valid for contrastive or triplet loss based networks, but cannot be transferred to classification networks trained by softmax-based losses.

5.4 Strategies Summary

Altogether, the center-based as well as the local inverted index based face sequence descriptors satisfy all technical requirements from section 5.1 which include track length independence, compactness and fast comparability. Both are specifically adjusted to the underlying face image descriptor. The local inverted index strategy includes an adaptation to the face domain in shape of the codebook learned from the unlabeled search database, which addresses the lack of domain specificity in the underlying LBP image descriptors. Improvements to the common inverted index strategy are made by constructing local indices on predefined image grid locations, which takes advantage of the face alignment. In comparison, the center-based face sequence descriptor exploits the properties of the CNN's discriminative target space induced by the proposed max-margin loss function which results in a simpler strategy because of the already highly specialized CNN-based face image descriptor. It is shown, that selecting the center to represent a face image sequence maximizes the inter-class distance.

Together, this means the unsupervised strategy learns the descriptor adaptation to the face domain on sequence level from unlabeled database samples, whereas the supervised strategy learns it on image level from labeled external face samples. In comparison with the center-based descriptor for the supervised strategy, the inverted index strategy is significantly more complex regarding the construction effort because it requires the initial creation of the codebook and inverted indices each time a new dataset is indexed. However, the face search is comparably efficient in both cases and on par with the most efficient alternatives from the literature.

6 Evaluation

The proposed strategies will be evaluated with regard to face verification and retrieval. Identification evaluation is ommitted in this thesis because it is directly related to verification under the closed world assumption as was shown in [Bol05]. While face retrieval is the final goal of this work and consequently evaluated in the final experiments, the verification setup will add the benefit of better understandable measures, more extensive comparison to related work and faster computation of results which is important for validation.

First, the evaluation protocols and the according measures will be presented. Next, the validation of all meta parameters is performed on validation datasets, which are distinct from the final test datasets. On this low-quality test data, the final evaluation will be performed in the last section of this chapter.

6.1 Measures and Methods

6.1.1 Face Verification

Each face verification method has to determine a similarity score $\mathcal{S}_{ij}$ judging the similarity of two provided face samples T_i and T_j. A higher score is supposed to indicate a higher likelihood for both face samples to originate from the same person.

For a score $\mathcal{S}_{ij}$ and a threshold θ, a matching identity is predicted if $\mathcal{S}_{ij} > \theta$:

$$\rho_{ij} = \begin{cases} 1 & \text{if } \mathcal{S}_{ij} > \theta \\ -1 & \text{otherwise} \end{cases} . \tag{6.1}$$

Depending on the values of the prediction ρ_{ij} and the indicator variable y_{ij}, for a test set of sample pairs, four outcomes are distinguished, as also illustrated in figure 6.1:

1. the true positives (*TP*) where $\rho_{ij} = y_{ij} = 1$ meaning the method correctly predicted the match,
2. the true negatives (*TN*) where $\rho_{ij} = y_{ij} = -1$ meaning the method correctly predicted the mismatch,
3. the false positives (*FP*) where $\rho_{ij} = 1$ and $y_{ij} = -1$ meaning the method falsely predicts a match for different identities and
4. the false negatives (*FN*) where $\rho_{ij} = -1$ and $y_{ij} = 1$ meaning the method falsely predicts a mismatch for the same identity.

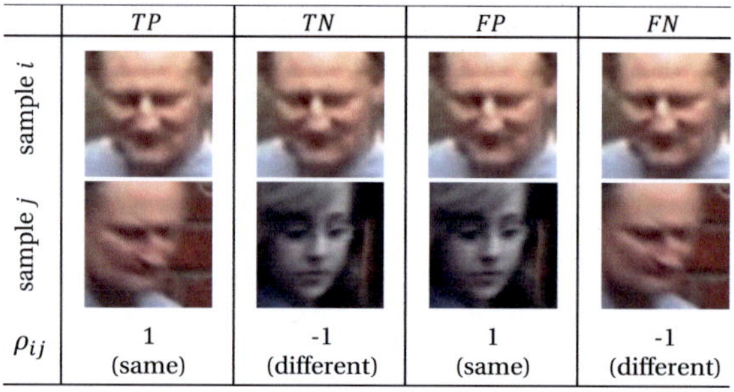

Figure 6.1: Illustration of *TP*, *TN*, *FP* and *FN*, where ρ_{ij} denotes the method's prediction.

Then plotting the true positive rate

$$TPR = \frac{TP}{TP + FN} \tag{6.2}$$

over the false positive rate

$$FPR = \frac{FP}{FP + TN} \tag{6.3}$$

yields the Receiver Operating Characteristic (ROC) curve if the threshold θ is varied over all occurring scores in the test set. There are two common options to reduce this curve into a single number which are the Area Under the Curve (AUC) and the Equal Error Rate (EER). While the AUC is self-explanatory, the EER denotes the *FPR* at the point of the curve where $FPR = FNR$ with the false negative rate $FNR = 1 - TPR$. Visually speaking, it is the intersection point of the ROC curve with the diagonal from the top left corner to the bottom right one in the diagram. The perfect AUC score is 1, whereas the best EER is 0.

In terms of practical applicability, the verification accuracy *acc*, defined as the percentage of correctly predicted pairs

$$acc = \frac{TP + TN}{TP + TN + FP + FN}, \tag{6.4}$$

is a simple and widespread measure. To determine the accuracy properly, the threshold θ has to be pre-selected on data different from the set of pairs the accuracy is calculated on. This allows to judge the transferability of the scores which is an import property in practical applications where pre-selection of the threshold is also required.

This motivates the application of a k-fold cross-validation for evaluation. Splitting the test dataset into k distinct folds with non-overlapping identities, testing on each fold allows to determine the threshold θ on the remaining $k-1$ folds. In addition, the statistical certainty of the measurement can be judged by the k separate cross-validation measurements for the accuracy. Serving this purpose, the accuracy's mean and standard deviation (*std*) will be denoted in all relevant cases. All following verification experiments will use $k = 10$ folds.

6.1.2 Face Retrieval

The retrieval performance is measured by the mean average precision *map* which is a standard performance measure for information retrieval tasks. It is widely spread for retrieval tasks across different applications [Agi06, Phi07a, Jég08, Bäu10].

Mean Average Precision

Given one query sample T_q, the quality of the score-based ranking Q_q of the N database samples T_i is assessed by the average precision:

$$ap = \sum_{j=1}^{N} Pr(j) \cdot \Delta Re(j), \tag{6.5}$$

with the precision $Pr(j)$ at rank j and the difference for the recall $\Delta Re(j)$ from rank $j-1$ to j: $\Delta Re(j) = Re(j) - Re(j-1)$. Recall $Re(j)$ and precision $Pr(j)$ result from the amount of true positives TP, false positives FP and false negatives FN on rank 1 to j:

$$Pr(j) = \frac{TP(j)}{TP(j) + FP(j)}, \tag{6.6}$$

$$Re(j) = \frac{TP(j)}{TP(j) + FN(j)}. \tag{6.7}$$

The precision quantifies the fraction of relevant search results within the top-j results while the recall quantifies which fraction of all matches are ranked in the top-j results. Thus, they measure the match density and completeness in the ranking.

The mean of m different queries to the database yields the mean average precision map:

$$map = \frac{1}{m} \sum_{i=1}^{m} ap_i. \tag{6.8}$$

Interpretation

The possible range for the average precision is $0 \leq ap \leq 1$. For $ap = 1$, all matching samples in the database having the query identity C_q are ranked at the topmost positions. The lower the matches are ranked, the lower the average precision becomes. An important property of the average precision is that it evaluates the positioning of all matches at once by aggregating it into a single scalar. Consequently, it measures the usability of the ranking for a human who will usually inspect the search result ranking from top to bottom to draw further conclusions such as occurrences of a specific person.

Two aspects are relevant in this case:

- It is better to have a larger number of matches near the top of the ranking instead of having one of several matches at the very top and the remaining ones far down in the ranking.
- It is only a minor flaw if a limited number of wrong results appear between the correct ones, because humans can usually filter and ignore them easily.

The *map* addresses both of these aspects and is consequently a good measure to judge the benefit of a search result for a human.

Database and Query Partitioning

Until now, it remained open how to gather the m queries. Existing face datasets define usually only a verification protocol which has to be followed if results should be compared with other approaches. However, the verification performance tells little about practical usability of a face recognition method in a retrieval scenario. To perform retrieval experiments, a dataset of N face samples is divided into k random but fixed splits whereof $k-1$ splits build the database and the face samples from the remaining split serve one-by-one as query samples. In k repetitions, each of the k splits will serve as query set. Altogether, this strategy results in equally many queries $m = N$ as the dataset has face samples. Two strategies for choosing k are common. Either the leave-one-out strategy with $k = N$ which maximizes data variety, or in resemblance of the verification cross-validation a strategy with $k = 10$. Reasons to choose less than N splits include computation intensive database preparations as in the case of the proposed inverted index strategy. In practical applications, the database has only to be constructed once which justifies a significant amount of preprocessing in this step. For a leave-one-out evaluation, however, the database must be constructed N times leading to an infeasibly high computational burden for large dataset evaluations.

In general, evaluation with the retrieval setup is significantly costlier than a verification setup which can be best seen at the YTF dataset example. The predefined official 10-fold cross-validation verification protocol includes altogether 5,000 track to track comparisons [Wol11]. Using a retrieval setup on the $N = 3{,}425$ tracks results in about 10 million track to track comparisons which forces methods to provide a significantly more efficient comparison strategy.

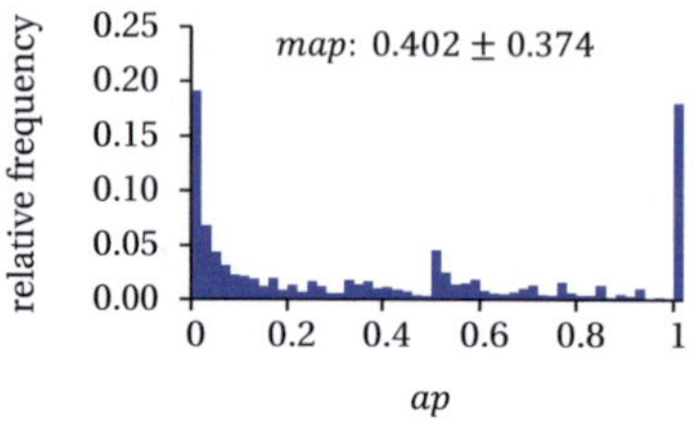

(a)

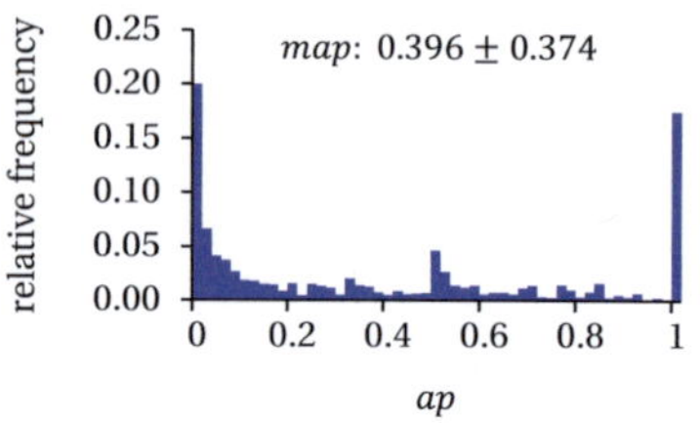

(b)

Figure 6.2: Typical average precision histograms for two different methods. A p-value of 0.0065 indicates a significant difference between both methods while standard deviation is insufficient. LqfNet combined with LMM (a) or MSM (b) on YTF.

Statistical Significance

In contrast to the verification protocol, where 10-fold cross-validation provides only a shallow statistical base for proving significant differences between methods, the retrieval protocol offers m query samples. But simply denoting the standard deviation in addition to the *map* is inappropriate because the average precision values ap_i are distributed asymmetrically and bound to the range [0,1], as illustrated for two examples in figure 6.2.

In consequence, significant differences between measured retrieval values for different methods are determined by a randomization test [Smu07]. This test checks the likelihood that a measured difference between two evaluated approaches is caused by one being better than the other instead of being mere coincidence. For this purpose, it tests if paired probes originate from the same base distribution. No assumptions about this distribution are necessary. Step by step, the test is performed as follows:

- The base for the decision are m paired probes in shape of the queries' average precisions ap_{i1} and ap_{i2} of both methods. They are called *paired* because for each query there exists a pair of measured average precisions, one from each method.
- Null hypothesis: Both methods are equally good. Thus the probes originate from the same base distribution $\mathcal{A}_i$ for each query: $ap_{i1} \sim \mathcal{A}_i$, $ap_{i2} \sim \mathcal{A}_i$.
- Basic idea: If the null hypothesis is valid, the assignment of a measurement to the respective method, meaning to switch ap_{i1} and ap_{i2}, would be irrelevant. Permutations would consequently have no influence on the evaluation measures.

- Test: Producing a large amount of random permutations and determining the respective tested measure which is the *map*. The p-value is the frequency over all permutations of a difference $|map_1 - map_2|$ at least as high as the original one.
- The null hypothesis is rejected if $p < \alpha$ with a selected significance level α of 0.05 which corresponds to a confidence of about two standard deviations.

In comparison to reporting only the mean and standard deviation of measurements, the randomization test has the advantage to statistically exploit the large number of queries which are performed in this experimental setup. Thus, it is capable of indicating smaller differences between retrieval algorithms as significant.

6.2 Available Data and Data Selection

Face data is required for several steps in the evaluation process.

- Training data is required for learning the CNN-based face image descriptor. Exploiting the advantage of the Siamese setup, the networks are trained on a combination of several large-scale face datasets including Celebrity-1000 [Liu14], FaceScrub [Ng14], MegaFace [Nec16], MSRA-CFW [Zha12a], TVC (section 3.5) and VGG Face dataset [Par15].
- Validation data is required to optimize meta-parameters of all image and sequence descriptors. The popular YTF dataset serves for sequence descriptor validation. In addition, this allows comparison of the results to further state-of-the-art approaches as well as human performance. However, some of the training datasets include identities also present in the YTF database. These identities are removed from the training set and serve as image validation set to avoid an identity overlap between training and validation data. Identities are assumed to be the same in case the celebrity names match with an edit distance of 1 or less. Table 6.1 lists all datasets including the relevant split sizes.
- As test data for the final low-quality experiments and comparison to other approaches two surveillance video face datasets are selected: the public ChokePoint [Won11] and the self-collected IOSB-SURV (section 3.5) dataset.

HR dataset faces are scaled by bilinear interpolation to the resolution stated at each experiment. As base resolution, face images are 32 × 32 pixels in size.

Table 6.1: Datasets and splits. Differences to official dataset sizes occur in case of images being no longer downloadable from internet links.

set	dataset name	#images	#sequences	#persons
train	Celebrities-1000 [Liu14]	2,117,837	145,751	930
	FaceScrub [Ng14]	51,162	51,162	451
	MegaFace [Nec16]	4,741,425	4,741,425	672,957
	MSRA [Zha12a]	163,018	163,018	1,372
	TV Collection [Her16c]	1,151,545	15,427	604
	VGG Face [Par15]	834,375	834,375	2,558
	combination	**9,059,362**	**5,951,158**	**678,872**
validation	Celebrities-1000 [Liu14]	210,154	13,981	70
	FaceScrub [Ng14]	10,299	10,299	79
	MSRA [Zha12a]	39,704	39,704	208
	combination	**260,157**	**63,984**	**357**
	YTF [Wol11]	621,126	3,425	1,595
test	ChokePoint [Won11]	63,570	1,278	29
	IOSB-SURV	366,664	5,011	138

6.3 Descriptor Training, Optimization and Validation

Each proposed method requires at least an optimization of the involved meta-parameters. In case of the supervised CNN face image descriptor, the model must also be trained. Both aspects will be covered in the following sections using a 10-fold verification setup. For the sake of clarity, detailed validation results are only shown for the case of 32 × 32 pixels faces. For further face sizes, only the final validation results are denoted. The proposed methods will be analyzed in detail on the validation data regarding their respective contribution to the final result.

6.3.1 Face Image Representations

To validate and optimize the face image representations, the combined validation face images from the Celebrities-1000, FaceScrub and MSRA-

CFW (MSRA) dataset will be used. With more than 250K images, the validation set offers a sufficient size. Because all face image descriptors $\mathcal{V}$ are understood as vectors in this section, they are denoted as $\boldsymbol{v}$. In the case of face image descriptors, the similarity score $\mathcal{S}(\boldsymbol{v}_1,\boldsymbol{v}_2)$ is the inverse vector distance $\mathcal{D}(\boldsymbol{v}_1,\boldsymbol{v}_2)$ between two image descriptors $\boldsymbol{v}_1$ and $\boldsymbol{v}_2$.

Table 6.2: Key LBP validation results for 32 × 32 pixels face size. Base settings are underlined.

parameter	case	value	*acc*	*std*
	1	1	0.572	0.015
	2	2	0.587	0.019
	3	3	0.596	0.017
regions l	<u>4</u>	4	0.608	0.018
	5	5	0.603	0.016
	6	6	0.607	0.013
	7	7	0.589	0.011
	8	4	0.597	0.013
	9	6	0.601	0.015
	10	8	0.606	0.016
points p	11	10	0.604	0.016
	<u>12</u>	12	0.608	0.018
	13	14	0.609	0.020
	14	0.5,-	0.605	0.018
	<u>15</u>	1,-	0.608	0.018
	16	1.5,-	0.609	0.016
	17	2,-	0.610	0.016
	18	2.5,-	0.572	0.018
	19	3,-	0.570	0.017
radii r_1,r_2	20	0.3,2	0.614	0.018
	21	0.5,2	0.615	0.018
	22	0.8,2	0.617	0.017
	23	1,2	0.617	0.015
	24	1,3	0.617	0.017
	25	2,3	0.606	0.016
	26	2	0.616	0.017
sampling density	<u>27</u>	4	0.617	0.017
δ for $r_1,r_2 = 1,2$	28	6	0.617	0.017
	29	8	0.616	0.016

Unsupervised LBP Descriptor

For the proposed unsupervised LR-LBP face image descriptor, the five meta-parameters

- l denoting the number of local regions in the grid in each dimension,
- p denoting the number of points extracted at
- radius r_1 around the LBP center point,
- density δ of radius samples between the inner radius r_1 and
- the outer radius r_2 with the radius step $\frac{r_2-r_1}{\delta-1}$,

are to be optimized. Image descriptor validation is performed with the concatenated local histogram feature vectors. Compared to HR applications where $l = 7$, $p = 8$, $r_1 = 2$, $r_2 = 2$ and $\delta = 1$ are a common choice [Aho06, Zou07a], fewer local regions and a smaller radius are expected to be a better solution. This intuition about the local regions l is confirmed on the validation set by table 6.2 (cases 1-7). In addition, it suggests a larger number of points around the center point (cases 8-13), although accuracy improvements beyond $p = 8$ are rather small and involve a significant increase in descriptor size. The baseline LBP radius options include only a single radius (cases 14-19). For the multi-scale histogram fusion, an equidistant sampling in δ steps between the lower radius r_1 and the upper radius r_2 (case 20-29) is chosen. Small radii are preferred as expected and it is shown that the proposed multi-scale histogram fusion strategy improves the baseline. This effect, albeit small, is consistent over all tested face resolutions but tends to decrease with higher resolutions, as indicated in figure 6.3. Because larger face images already offer more patterns per local region, the benefit of the additional patterns generated by multi-scale histogram fusion is expected to decrease. Also, the overall accuracy increases consistently up to about 28×28 pixels face size. Above this size, first signs of performance saturation can be observed.

Table 6.3: Multi-scale LBP validation results.

multi-scale strategy	*acc*	*std*
none	0.608	0.018
histogram fusion	0.617	0.015
image pyramid (regular)	0.602	0.026
image pyramid (radius scales)	0.595	0.022
histogram fusion + image pyramid (regular)	0.611	0.020

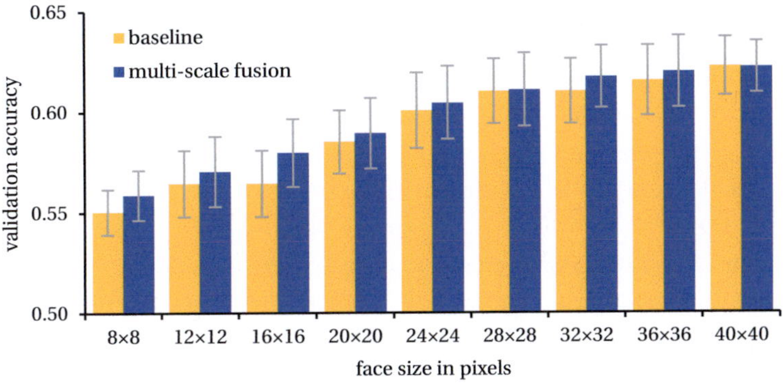

Figure 6.3: Resolution dependence of LBP validation performance. Indicators denote one standard deviation in each direction.

Regarding different methods to incorporate multi-scale information, a comparison between the proposed multi-scale fusion strategy and a baseline feature extraction from an image pyramid (section 4.1.2) is performed. Note that using the image pyramid leads to higher dimensional image descriptors caused by the additional regions in the new scales. Chosen scales are either face widths

- $\hat{w}_s = \lambda^{-s} \cdot \hat{w}$ for $\lambda = 1.2$ and $s = 0,\dots,3$ representing a regular image pyramid, or
- $\hat{w}_s = \lambda_s \cdot \hat{w}$ with $\lambda_s = 1, \frac{3}{4}, \frac{3}{5}, \frac{1}{2}$ to exactly match the radius scales of the fusion strategy.

In comparison to the improvement by the proposed histogram fusion, all image pyramid based solutions in table 6.3 perform worse. Especially, they perform even worse than the baseline solution having no scale strategy.

Supervised CNN Descriptor

The learning of CNN-based face image descriptors for the proposed supervised strategy is a process including several steps. The conducted steps to obtain the final network configurations are:

1. The best network architectures are found by a meta-parameter and architecture optimization process. Due to memory limitations, this is performed without the MegaFace and VGG Face training datasets. After empiric determination of a potential parameter optimum for

each architecture type, a systematic optimization starting from this configuration is performed in each case to further improve the network structure into the final configuration. These networks are called Low-Resolution Face Networks (LrfNets).

2. Appropriate training data augmentations are determined to reduce the domain gap to low-quality data. LrfNets trained with an augmentation strategy will be called Low-Quality Face Networks (LqfNets).
3. For each architecture type, two final versions will be trained from scratch on all training datasets with and without training data augmentations, leading to three LrfNets and three LqfNets.

Each training batch $\mathcal{B}$ consists of 100 image pairs, half positive and half negative ones. The pairs in a batch are sampled from the different training datasets in a fixed ratio to benefit from the data diversity in each training iteration. All networks are trained from scratch using Caffe [Jia14]. Table 6.4 shows selected results for key parameters on architecture optimization. The filter number G is given for the first 3×3 convolutional layer and doubled after each layer group. Several observation can be made:

- Notable differences are observed for the number of fully connected layers at the end of the network (case 13-15). At least one is required in the classical and exactly one in the residual architecture. The results for the inception architecture are inconclusive with no or two fully connected layers performing comparably and, in the sense of reducing parameters, it is preferred to choose none. The differing results can be explained by the varying capabilities of the respective architecture blocks in front.
- Analysis of the descriptor dimension d confirms previous findings from related literature with $d = 128$ performing best overall (case 21-25) [Sch15b, Sim13, Par14]. Only the inception architecture appears to require slightly more target dimensions for the best embedding.
- Meta-parameters influencing the network size, such as G or H, behave largely as expected where increasing the number of network parameters improves the results up to a range where saturation is observed. In theory, even further increases should lead to overfitting and decreasing validation results in all these cases. Hardware limitations prevented to clearly verify this in all cases. Only for the number of neurons per fully connected layer H the effect becomes visible.

Table 6.4: Key validation results of the systematical architecture optimization. Base settings for each architecture and parameter are underlined. Missing values are caused by insufficient GPU memory.

parameter	case	value	classical		residual		inception	
			acc	*std*	*acc*	*std*	*acc*	*std*
input color space	1	gray	0.776	0.010	0.758	0.009	0.772	0.013
	2	RGB	0.742	0.014	0.695	0.004	0.766	0.012
# groups N_g	3	2	0.771	0.013	0.664	0.006	0.754	0.011
	4	3	0.776	0.010	0.758	0.009	0.772	0.013
	5	4	0.789	0.010	0.770	0.009	0.657	0.008
# filters G	6	64	0.687	0.014	0.758	0.009	0.728	0.008
	7	128	0.771	0.013	0.762	0.007	0.755	0.015
	8	192	0.784	0.018	0.760	0.012	0.772	0.013
	9	256	0.776	0.010	0.762	0.009	0.778	0.011
	10	384	0.784	0.009	-	-	0.737	0.112
	11	512	0.786	0.013	-	-	-	-
	12	768	0.795	0.012	-	-	-	-
# fully connected layers N_f	13	0	0.767	0.010	0.719	0.004	0.772	0.013
	14	1	0.776	0.010	0.758	0.009	0.732	0.013
	15	2	0.779	0.012	0.641	0.009	0.777	0.008
# neurons per fully connected layer H	16	512	0.762	0.004	0.717	0.006	0.726	0.010
	17	1024	0.782	0.012	0.761	0.010	0.732	0.013
	18	2048	0.776	0.010	0.758	0.009	0.693	0.015
	19	4096	0.781	0.011	0.765	0.006	0.636	0.022
	20	8192	0.759	0.014	0.700	0.010	0.581	0.018
descriptor dimension d	21	64	0.629	0.016	0.745	0.008	0.704	0.014
	22	96	0.760	0.016	0.747	0.010	0.741	0.011
	23	128	0.776	0.010	0.758	0.009	0.772	0.013
	24	192	0.754	0.016	0.740	0.016	0.775	0.009
	25	256	0.713	0.013	0.718	0.011	0.742	0.012
loss function L	26	contrastive	0.752	0.009	0.627	0.010	0.632	0.021
	27	triplet	0.776	0.010	0.661	0.023	0.740	0.009
	28	max-margin	0.776	0.010	0.758	0.009	0.772	0.013

- The proposed max-margin loss significantly outperforms the contrastive loss and, especially for the modern architectures, also the triplet loss (case 26-28). Learning rates are optimized individually for each loss and are $\psi = 0.0001$ for max-margin and triplet, and $\psi = 0.001$ for contrastive.
- Probably the most counter-intuitive result is that including color information (case 2) leads to worse results. Humans usually have the perception that face matching relies significantly on skin color. However, having a closer look, skin color is in most cases only a hint to ethnicity which simultaneously manifests in the face shape leading to redundant information. This can easily be illustrated with a synthetic face model which allows to adjust the face shape independently of face color and texture. Figure 6.4 shows three renderings with the FaceGen face modeling tool[1] which allows to change the ethnicity of a face without changing further parameters. Thus, the face models with only the shape differing between African, European and East Asian ethnicity are generated. Despite having the same color, the differences are still prominent in the shape and easily distinguishable. This explains why adding color information deteriorates the results because input image dimension is increased by a factor of three with no additional content information included. Or put the other way round: transformation to gray-scale offers a dimension reduction by factor three without losing task specific information.

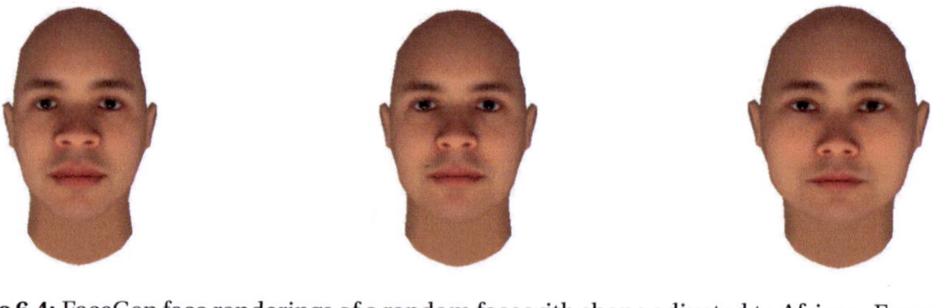

Figure 6.4: FaceGen face renderings of a random face with shape adjusted to African, European and East Asian ethnicity (left to right).

[1] https://facegen.com/modeller.htm

- Overall, the classical architecture performs best with the inception architecture coming close and the residual one being slightly worse. This indicates that architectures allowing deeper networks are inferior for LR applications compared to the classical concept. It appears that the LR images contain too few information to feed a very deep network.
- Finally, the differences in validation accuracy near the optimum are mostly below the measured standard deviation. So from a statistical viewpoint, the measurement noise on the accuracy justifies the choice of a meta-parameter setting which appears to be slightly off the maximum. This becomes relevant if runtime and memory consumption have to be considered along with the matching performance.

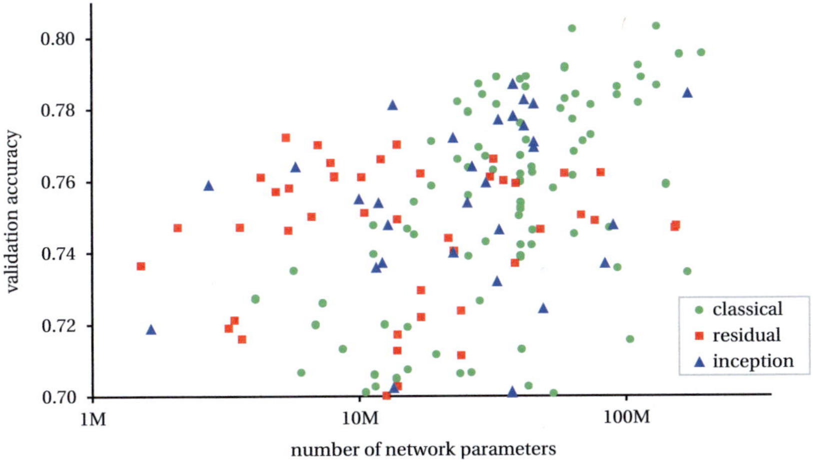

Figure 6.5: Validation accuracy vs. number of network parameters for LrfNets.

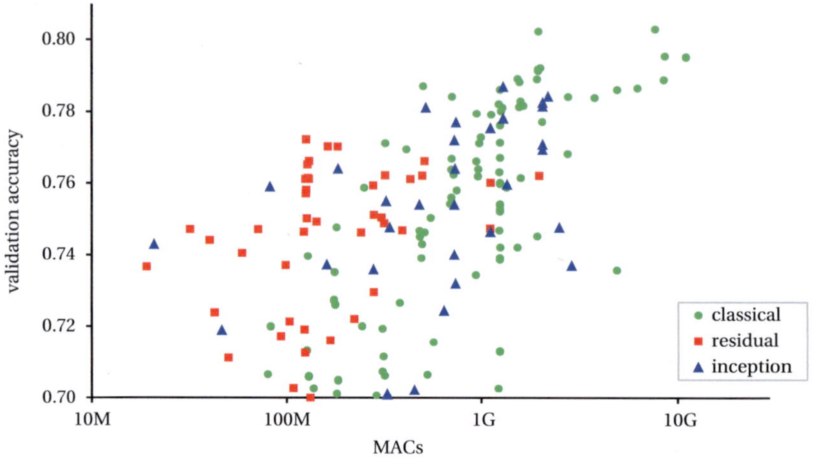

Figure 6.6: Validation accuracy vs. network MACs for LrfNets.

One of the main differences between the classical architecture and the modern residual and inception one is the number of parameters and the respective dependence thereon to achieve a good accuracy. The modern architectures require less parameters to achieve a comparable performance as figure 6.5 indicates, which includes all trained networks above 0.7 accuracy. In addition, there is weak correlation of 0.44 between the number of the parameters and the accuracy for the classical architecture whereas residual (0.27) and inception (-0.10) show less or almost no correlation. The same holds for the relation between required network Multiply-and-Accumulates (MACs) and performance (see figure 6.6). But the stated number of MACs is only a theoretical value regarding the required operations to process one face image. In practice, execution times increase significantly with network depth due to relatively higher memory usage by the large amount of intermediate layers. Tables 6.5 and 6.6 show the properties for the best LrfNet of each architecture including measured execution times on an Nvidia Titan X GPU. Note that despite having the most MACs, the classical network's inference is the fastest due to less required memory operations.

Regarding the input resolution of face images, figure 6.7 offers valuable clues. For each network input size, an architecture optimization is performed and the results for the optimized networks are shown. In detail the findings are:

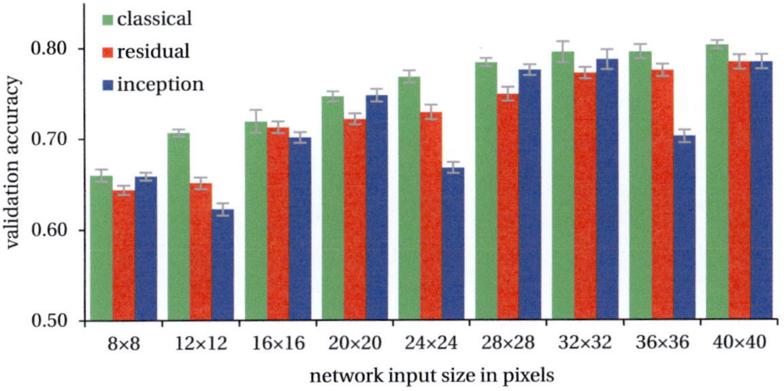

Figure 6.7: Resolution dependence of CNN validation performance. Indicators denote one standard deviation in each direction.

- In general, the performance relation between architecture types remains stable across resolutions.
- The inception network performance drops significantly for face widths which are a multiple of 12 pixels. Further analysis of this effect provided no solid evidence of the reason. An unfortunate influence between the different scale paths in the inception block is suspected.
- Significant performance improvements are observed for resolutions up to 28×28 pixels. Afterwards, first signs of saturation appear with further improvements becoming smaller.
- The CNN performance for the smallest face resolution of 8×8 pixels already surpasses the performance of all unsupervised LBP face image descriptors from figure 6.3. A significant aspect on that matter is the validation with downscaled HR face images which significantly reduces noise. In relation, in-the-wild face images captured at this resolution include significantly more noise and other quality degrading effects. Thus, this performance represents an upper bound of what the CNN and LBP face image descriptors are capable of at this very low resolution.

Table 6.5: Final, optimized network structures. Notation is similar to [He15a], where layer size denotes receptive field size (pool), receptive field size and number of filters (conv), or number of neurons (fc).

classical

layer type	size	stride, pad
conv	3×3×512	1,1
conv	3×3×512	1,1
pool	3×3	2,0
conv	3×3×1024	1,1
pool	3×3	2,0
conv	3×3×2048	1,1
pool	3×3	2,0
fc	2048	
fc	128	

residual

layer type	size	stride, pad
conv	3×3×128	1,1
pool	2×2	2,0
residual	$\begin{bmatrix}3\times3\times128\\3\times3\times128\end{bmatrix}$	$\begin{bmatrix}1,1\\1,1\end{bmatrix}$
residual	$\begin{bmatrix}3\times3\times128\\3\times3\times128\end{bmatrix}$	$\begin{bmatrix}1,1\\1,1\end{bmatrix}$
residual	$\begin{bmatrix}3\times3\times256\\3\times3\times256\end{bmatrix}$	$\begin{bmatrix}2,1\\1,1\end{bmatrix}$
residual	$\begin{bmatrix}3\times3\times256\\3\times3\times256\end{bmatrix}$	$\begin{bmatrix}1,1\\1,1\end{bmatrix}$
residual	$\begin{bmatrix}3\times3\times512\\3\times3\times512\end{bmatrix}$	$\begin{bmatrix}2,1\\1,1\end{bmatrix}$
residual	$\begin{bmatrix}3\times3\times512\\3\times3\times512\end{bmatrix}$	$\begin{bmatrix}1,1\\1,1\end{bmatrix}$
fc	4096	
fc	128	

inception

layer type	size	stride, pad
conv	3×3×224	1,1
pool	3×3	2,0
inception	$\begin{bmatrix}\begin{bmatrix}1\times1\times224\end{bmatrix}\\\begin{bmatrix}1\times1\times224\\3\times3\times448\end{bmatrix}\\\begin{bmatrix}1\times1\times56\\3\times3\times112\\3\times3\times112\end{bmatrix}\\\begin{bmatrix}\text{pool}3\times3\\1\times1\times112\end{bmatrix}\end{bmatrix}$	$\begin{bmatrix}1,0\\1,0\\1,1\\1,0\\1,1\\1,1\\1,1\\1,0\end{bmatrix}$
pool	3×3	2,0
inception	$\begin{bmatrix}\begin{bmatrix}1\times1\times448\end{bmatrix}\\\begin{bmatrix}1\times1\times448\\3\times3\times896\end{bmatrix}\\\begin{bmatrix}1\times1\times112\\3\times3\times224\\3\times3\times224\end{bmatrix}\\\begin{bmatrix}\text{pool}3\times3\\1\times1\times224\end{bmatrix}\end{bmatrix}$	$\begin{bmatrix}1,0\\1,0\\1,1\\1,0\\1,1\\1,1\\1,1\\1,0\end{bmatrix}$
pool	3×3	2,0
inception	$\begin{bmatrix}\begin{bmatrix}1\times1\times896\end{bmatrix}\\\begin{bmatrix}1\times1\times896\\3\times3\times1792\end{bmatrix}\\\begin{bmatrix}1\times1\times224\\3\times3\times448\\3\times3\times448\end{bmatrix}\\\begin{bmatrix}\text{pool}3\times3\\1\times1\times448\end{bmatrix}\end{bmatrix}$	$\begin{bmatrix}1,0\\1,0\\1,1\\1,0\\1,1\\1,1\\1,1\\1,0\end{bmatrix}$
pool	3×3	2,0
fc	128	

Table 6.6: Final network configurations. Configuration denotes case numbers in table 6.4.

	classical	residual	inception
configuration (cases)	1,4,11,14,18,22,27	1,4,7,14,18,22,27	1,4,8-9,13,22,27
validation accuracy *acc*	0.786	0.766	0.787
parameters	74.1M	32.0M	29.2M
MACs	1,279M	512M	986M
prediction time (ms)	2.1	4.2	6.4
memory footprint (MB)	338	230	239

Table 6.7: Benefit of the training data augmentations.

effect	no augmentation (LrfNet)		with augmentation (LqfNet)	
	acc	*std*	*acc*	*std*
none	0.786	0.005	-	-
flip	0.780	0.004	0.780	0.005
crop	0.765	0.006	0.775	0.005
rotation	0.777	0.006	0.775	0.005
motion blur	0.695	0.008	0.747	0.004
noise	0.753	0.006	0.772	0.007
compression	0.756	0.003	0.762	0.004
rescale	0.778	0.006	0.775	0.003

To address the low-quality aspects of surveillance data, quality augmentation strategies were proposed in section 4.2.2 to close the gap to the target domain. Because the number of low-quality datasets is limited and both available ones will serve as final test sets, network validation is performed with synthetically adjusted versions of the validation face images. This also offers the opportunity to assess each effect separately whereas in-the-wild data always includes a blend of quality degrading effects. The validation data is synthetically degraded with the same strategy as the training data in the augmentation process. Note that because of the probabilistic change of image quality, verification includes comparison of face pairs which may both be degraded, unchanged or one degraded while the other is not, all with different strengths of degradation being possible.

Table 6.7 first denotes the influence of the different geometric and image quality effects on the validation results for the classical LrfNet. The most significant performance loss is observed for motion blur. In comparison, isotropic blur, as included in the anti-aliasing filters for rescaling, has a far lower influence. Image noise, compression artifacts and bad face alignment resulting in non-optimally cropped faces are further effects where a significant performance loss is observed, albeit smaller than in the motion blur case. Flipping, rotation and rescaling artifacts have only a minor influence.

In the second step, an LqfNet is trained for each effect with the according training data augmentation strategy and compared to the otherwise identical non-augmented LrfNet. Depending on the previously observed influence, the augmentation strategies show different results. In case the degrading effect has only a minor influence, the augmentation causes only irrelevant performance changes. However, in the cases where results are significantly affected, especially for motion blur, the training data augmentation regains large parts of the lost performance. All in all, the final LqfNet for each architecture is consequently trained with the combination of the crop, motion blur, noise and compression training data augmentation. The final networks are trained at this point with the full combined training data including MegaFace and VGG Face, and remain fixed in the following sections. Note that no transfer learning in the shape of dataset fine-tuning will be performed in any case for the LrfNet and LqfNet descriptors later on. This will show the generalization capabilities of the trained networks.

Baseline and Vector Distances

For the previously unspecified vector distance $\mathcal{D}(\boldsymbol{v}_1,\boldsymbol{v}_2)$, three choices are considered: Euclidean, Cosine and Hellinger [Wol08, Ara12d]. Furthermore, the set of baseline face image descriptors will be presented together with an evaluation of the according vector distance $\mathcal{D}$.

Cosine and Hellinger distance can be computed by preprocessing the vectors $\boldsymbol{v}$ by either normalizing their length

$$\boldsymbol{v}_c = \frac{\boldsymbol{v}}{||\boldsymbol{v}||} \tag{6.9}$$

for Cosine, or element-wise signed square rooting

$$v_{j,h} = \text{sign}(v_j) \cdot \sqrt{|v_j|} \tag{6.10}$$

for Hellinger distance and afterwards applying the Euclidean distance

$$\mathcal{D}_e(\boldsymbol{v}_1,\boldsymbol{v}_2) = ||\boldsymbol{v}_1 - \boldsymbol{v}_2||_2 \,. \tag{6.11}$$

The Hellinger distance $\mathcal{D}_h$ is common for distributions [Pol02] and as such expected and known to work well for histogram-based feature vectors [Wol08, Ara12d]. The normalization of the Cosine distance $\mathcal{D}_c$ is, for example, beneficial in the case of pixel intensity descriptors as it yields a certain illumination robustness.

Considering these facts, for the proposed LBP and CNN descriptors the Hellinger and the Euclidean distance are expected to be the best fit because of the histogram character in the first and the Euclidean-based loss function in the second case. Table 6.8 confirms this largely and indicates further the appropriate distances for the baseline face image descriptors. These descriptors are the raw vectorized pixel intensities, the dense SIFT descriptor [Sim13] and the state-of-the-art HR CNN-based VGG Face image descriptor [Par15]. LR face images are upsampled to the fixed CNN input size of 224 × 224 pixels for the VGG Face image descriptor.

Further, the results for different image descriptors in table 6.8 indicate that CNN-based descriptors significantly outperform conventional solutions such as local features (LBP, dense SIFT) on the high quality validation data. Also, an adapted CNN is important for a good LR performance, because applying the HR VGG Face network leads to significantly worse results than the best proposed LR architectures. The 3-5% performance improvement for the CNN-based image descriptors compared to the previous section (table 6.6) originates from the additional data in the MegaFace and VGG Face datasets which were added for final network training.

Table 6.8: Vector distance selection for face image descriptors based on validation results.

	Cosine		Euclidean		Hellinger	
	acc	*std*	*acc*	*std*	*acc*	*std*
LR-LBP	0.613	0.017	0.602	0.012	**0.617**	0.015
LrfNet classical	0.818	0.019	**0.818**	0.016	0.809	0.017
LrfNet residual	0.800	0.021	**0.796**	0.019	0.785	0.021
LrfNet inception	0.840	0.019	**0.839**	0.020	0.820	0.017
LqfNet classical	0.830	0.014	**0.834**	0.017	0.835	0.011
LqfNet residual	0.752	0.018	**0.758**	0.019	0.751	0.020
LqfNet inception	0.764	0.016	**0.795**	0.017	0.782	0.011
VGG Face [Par15]	**0.803**	0.012	0.702	0.024	0.756	0.019
dense SIFT [Sim13]	**0.558**	0.025	0.527	0.025	0.553	0.026
$LBP^{u2}_{8,2}$ [Aho06]	0.595	0.016	0.601	0.012	**0.602**	0.014
raw pixel	**0.558**	0.025	0.527	0.025	0.553	0.026

6.3.2 Face Sequence Representations

Sequence descriptor validation experiments are performed with high-quality but LR data in the shape of a 32 × 32 pixels version of the YTF dataset.

Table 6.9: Validation results for inverted index based methods. p-value significance indicators are in relation to the respectively previous case.

parameter	**case**	**value**	**global index (baseline)**		**local indices (proposed)**	
			map	$p < 0.05$	*map*	$p < 0.05$
codebook size K	1	32,000	0.020	-	0.053	-
	2	64,000	0.023	✓	0.056	✓
	3	128,000	0.028	✓	0.059	✓
	4	256,000	0.030	✓	0.062	✓
	5	512,000	0.032	✓	0.063	
	6	1,024,000	-	-	0.064	
feature augmentation for $K = 64000$	7	none	0.023		0.056	
	8	pose	0.023		0.056	
	9	location	0.040	✓	-	
	10	encoded	0.041	✓	-	

Inverted Index Descriptor

The validation of the proposed unsupervised inverted index approach combined with the LR-LBP image descriptor is performed with the retrieval setup because it is unsuitable for face verification. The inverted index method includes two key components where fast algorithms are necessary. First, the clustering of a large dataset to build the codebook and secondly, the nearest neighbor search to assign the corresponding visual word to a feature. The VLFeat library [Ved08] is applied in both cases because it provides efficient algorithms based on KD-trees [Fri77, Bei97].

Table 6.9 indicates that:

- Increasing the codebook size (cases 1-6) significantly improves the performance up to the range of half a million visual words. Remember that in the case of the proposed strategy of local indices, the denoted codebook size is equally distributed among all local indices reducing computational complexity compared to the global approach and making larger codebooks possible.
- Moving from a global index (left) to the proposed local index strategy (right) improves the results significantly due to the strictly enforced separation of features from different face locations.
- When comparing the local index strategy to feature augmentation by feature location as proposed in related literature [Li13, Par14, Sim13]

(case 9), the performance benefit of the local index strategy becomes clearly obvious.

- The proposed feature pose augmentation, presented in section 4.1.3, leading to a complete feature encoding when combined with location augmentation, yields small improvements which are significant in one case according to the randomization test (cases 8+10).

For further experiments, this validation suggests a final codebook of size $K = 256{,}000$ because further performance improvements are insignificant but inflict higher computational costs.

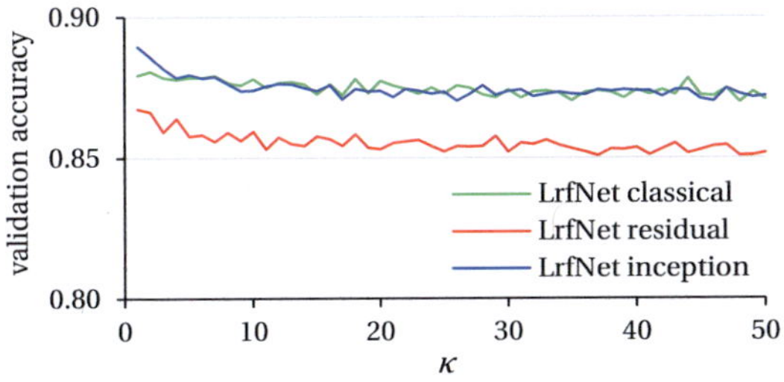

Figure 6.8: Influence of an increasing number of local means κ for the proposed LMM track descriptor on YTF accuracy.

Center-based Descriptor

Only the parameter κ denoting the number of centers requires consideration for the proposed center-based LMM sequence descriptor to be combined with the CNN-based face image descriptors in the supervised strategy. While the intuitive motivation in section 5.3.1 for the proposed center-based sequence descriptor gave no theoretical hint for the choice of κ except $\kappa < n$ for n frames in a sequence, the theoretical loss-based motivation in section 5.3.2 fixes $\kappa = 1$. In particular, following this motivation, a larger κ should have potentially negative influence because the centers start to move to the border of the identity set. This behavior is empirically confirmed for all LrfNet descriptors in figure 6.8. For comparison to the results of the inverted index approach, the retrieval result of the best option of figure 6.8 is a *map* of 0.390 which indicates a clear superiority of the supervised approach on this kind of data.

Baseline and Combinations

This section serves two purposes: First, to show that the theoretical motivations for the proposed center-based sequence descriptor yield practical benefits and, second, to compare the proposed supervised strategy to baseline methods. This will lead to a comparison with published state-of-the-art results on the YTF dataset in the next section. Because comparative experiments on YTF have to stick to the official verification protocol, the unsupervised inverted index strategy will be omitted here because it works only for retrieval. The LR-LBP image descriptor will instead be combined with the best verification sequence descriptor.

Comparison of the LrfNet and LqfNet face image descriptors is performed with the state-of-the-art HR CNN VGG Face image descriptor [Par15], as well as the local feature based LBP [Aho06] and dense SIFT [Sim13] face image descriptors, and raw vectorized pixel data.

The proposed center-based track descriptor distance $\mathcal{D}(\mathcal{W}_1,\mathcal{W}_2)$ is compared with the two *set-based* track distances, minset (nearest neighbor)

$$\mathcal{D}_m(\mathcal{W}_1,\mathcal{W}_2) = \min_{\boldsymbol{v}_1\in\mathcal{W}_1,\boldsymbol{v}_2\in\mathcal{W}_2} \mathcal{D}(\boldsymbol{v}_1,\boldsymbol{v}_2), \tag{6.12}$$

and best-shot

$$\mathcal{D}_b(\mathcal{W}_1,\mathcal{W}_2) = \mathcal{D}(\boldsymbol{v}_1^b,\boldsymbol{v}_2^b) \tag{6.13}$$

distance, where $\mathcal{D}$ denotes the appropriate vector distance, $\mathcal{W}_i$ the set of face image descriptors $\boldsymbol{v}_i$ from a face sequence and $\boldsymbol{v}_i^b$ the descriptor of the best face image in the respective face track in terms of most frontal head pose. MSM [Fuk05] as *space-based* and LLE [Had09c] as *manifold-based* method, together with the *set-based* ones, are compared to the proposed track descriptor method.

The choice regarding the face sequence distance $\mathcal{D}(\mathcal{W}_1,\mathcal{W}_2)$ has a significant impact on the practicability of video face matching because it heavily influences comparison complexity, as indicated in table 2.2. For full reference, table 6.10 lists the verification results for all image and sequence descriptor combinations. As theoretically expected, some combinations work better than others.

- While the slow minset distance $\mathcal{D}_m$ shows the best results for the conventional descriptors (pixel, LBP, dense SIFT) in accordance with previous findings [Che11b, Wol11], this is different for CNN face image descriptors (LrfNet, LqfNet, VGG Face).
- In the context of CNNs, the proposed LMM sequence descriptor is the favorable choice because matching face tracks is as fast as with the best-shot method, while also achieving superior or comparable performance compared with all other methods.
- Only MSM rivals LMM for matching performance in this case which is caused by its concept of representing a face track as a linear subspace. This involves a beneficial averaging effect similar to the proposed LMM. However, it involves a higher computational overhead leading to slower comparison.

Altogether, this means that the proposed supervised system achieves a superior performance on YTF with a face track descriptor of only 128 dimensions where comparison can be efficiently performed by Euclidean distance.

Table 6.10: Comparison of face image and track descriptor combinations on YTF validation dataset for verification setup.

	acc±*std*				
	best shot	minset	MSM	LLE	*LMM*
raw pixel	0.551±0.019	**0.604±0.030**	0.583±0.028	0.513±0.022	0.582±0.024
dense SIFT	0.584±0.016	**0.656±0.007**	0.622±0.011	0.516±0.021	0.636±0.015
LR-LBP	0.596±0.021	**0.652±0.017**	0.632±0.021	0.521±0.018	0.623±0.014
VGG-Face	0.795±0.009	0.854±0.010	0.857±0.011	0.521±0.020	**0.859±0.011**
LrfNet classical	0.832±0.017	0.873±0.011	0.878±0.016	0.542±0.024	**0.879±0.019**
LrfNet residual	0.810±0.022	0.850±0.014	**0.871±0.021**	0.619±0.020	0.867±0.022
LrfNet inception	0.842±0.016	0.870±0.019	0.888±0.018	0.592±0.020	**0.889±0.016**
LqfNet classical	0.855±0.018	0.891±0.015	0.874±0.016	0.565±0.015	**0.901±0.012**
LqfNet residual	0.776±0.020	0.817±0.021	0.838±0.019	0.611±0.017	**0.839±0.021**
LqfNet inception	0.831±0.014	0.852±0.016	0.859±0.016	0.652±0.019	**0.866±0.012**

Comparison to YTF State-of-the-Art Results

Despite YTF being a very popular dataset for face verification experiments, LR results on this dataset are rare. Nevertheless, comparison is performed to the few published LR results in table 6.11 in addition to the self-implemented baseline LR approaches. Note that the only competing approach, the SRFR-NET [Wu16], achieving 0.907 accuracy on a 27×31 pixel version, is based on a significantly larger and more complex network with 224×224 pixels input size with an image upscaling part in front of it and a target descriptor four times the size of the LrfNets and LqfNets to achieve a comparable performance. This results in a much slower descriptor computation and comparison.

As expected, state-of-the-art HR results on YTF are still superior because of more visible face details at the original face size which is about 100×100 pixels. Nevertheless, the achieved LR performance is in the range of human accuracy on the original HR YTF data which was reported to be 0.897 on average [BR14].

Table 6.11: Comparison of baseline and proposed LR approaches to published state-of-the-art results on the YTF dataset on different modalities.

category	**method**	**face size in pixels**	*acc*	*std*	AUC	EER
proposed LR	*LR-LBP* + minset	32×32	0.652	0.017	0.701	0.356
	LqfNet classical + LMM	32×32	**0.901**	0.012	0.966	0.100
baseline LR	raw pixel + minset	32×32	0.604	0.030	0.639	0.406
	dense SIFT + minset	32×32	0.656	0.007	0.719	0.340
	VGG-Face + LMM	32×32	**0.859**	0.011	0.933	0.144
LR	SRFRNET [Wu16]	27×31	**0.907**	-	-	-
	DARG [Wan15]	24×40	-	-	0.730	-
HR	FaceNet [Sch15b]	original	**0.951**	0.004	-	-
	VGG-Face [Par15]	original	0.916	-	-	-
	DeepFace [Tai14]	original	0.914	0.011	0.963	0.086
	VF^2 [Par14]	original	0.847	0.014	0.930	0.149
	MBGS [Wol11]	original	0.764	0.018	0.869	0.212
	LBP + minset [Wol11]	original	0.657	0.017	0.707	0.352
human [BR14]	average	original	0.897	-	-	-
	familiar faces	original	**0.935**	-	-	-
	unfamiliar faces	original	0.831	-	-	-

6.3.3 Validation Summary

The validation process presented the optimization of the meta-parameters for all proposed approaches. Key findings include that the LBP histogram fusion boosts performance with decreasing face resolution and that the local inverted index compares favorably to a global inverted index. In addition, the systematic CNN optimization improved results significantly and resulted in a compact network which achieves state-of-the-art performance on a LR version of the YTF dataset. Finally, the proposed center-based sequence descriptor has proven to be the best overall choice for CNN-based face image descriptors. Only the training dataset augmentation showed mixed results on the high-quality validation data, this can be assessed more accurately in the following low-quality target domain tests.

6.4 Experiments

After choosing the final optimized settings for each approach in the last section, the experiments on the in-the-wild surveillance test datasets ChokePoint and IOSB-SURV serve as final challenge for the proposed video-to-video face matching strategies. Both, verification and retrieval results will be denoted. The experiments are completed by a distinct comparison to prove the benefits of the contributions in this thesis.

Remember that even though the ChokePoint dataset is captured in a surveillance scenario including the challenges such as illumination and pose variations, the image quality is still high for at least a few frames per sequence caused by the camera setup. 63 percent of ChokePoint sequences include a face of at least 100×100 pixels whereas only 23 percent of IOSB-SURV sequences do.

6.4.1 Comparative Experiments

Testing the proposed approaches as well as the baseline ones in a verification setup yields convincing results in table 6.12 for the proposed supervised strategy on both datasets. Figures 6.9 and 6.10 depict the according ROC-curves, limited to the classical CNN architecture for clarity. Significant improvements compared to the baseline methods are observed and further observations are:

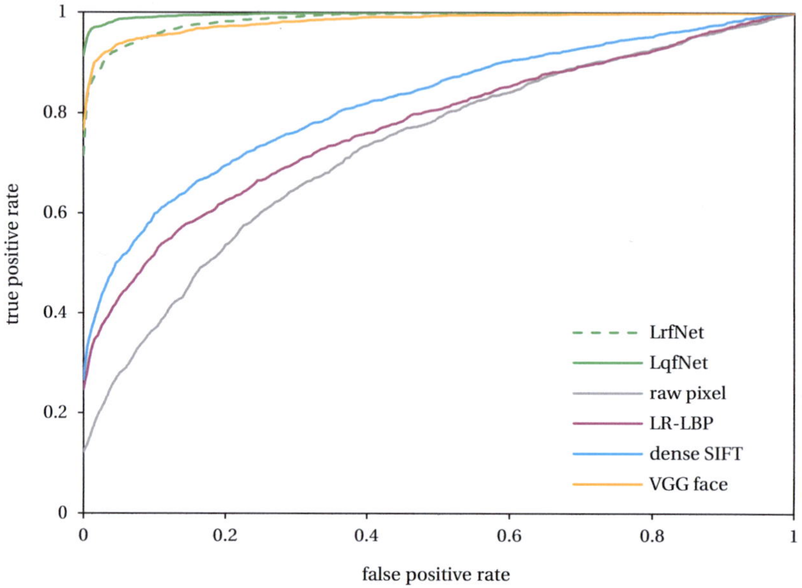

Figure 6.9: ROC-curves on Chokepoint test set. Only classical LrfNet and LqfNet are shown.

- The improvements for the proposed augmentation strategy are minor, if existing at all, for the ChokePoint results, similar to the high-quality validation results in the previous section. In case of actual low-quality data as represented by IOSB-SURV, the benefit becomes obvious, especially, for the classical architecture. The data augmentation strategy compensates the significant motion blur and noise in the data well.
- While no major differences between the architectures can be observed for the LrfNets, the classical one is the best in combination with the data augmentation in shape of the LqfNet.

The practical usage of the proposed face matching strategies on the target scenario is demonstrated with the retrieval protocol. The average duration t_q for a query is measured in addition to the *map*. Significant differences regarding this aspect become obvious in table 6.13.

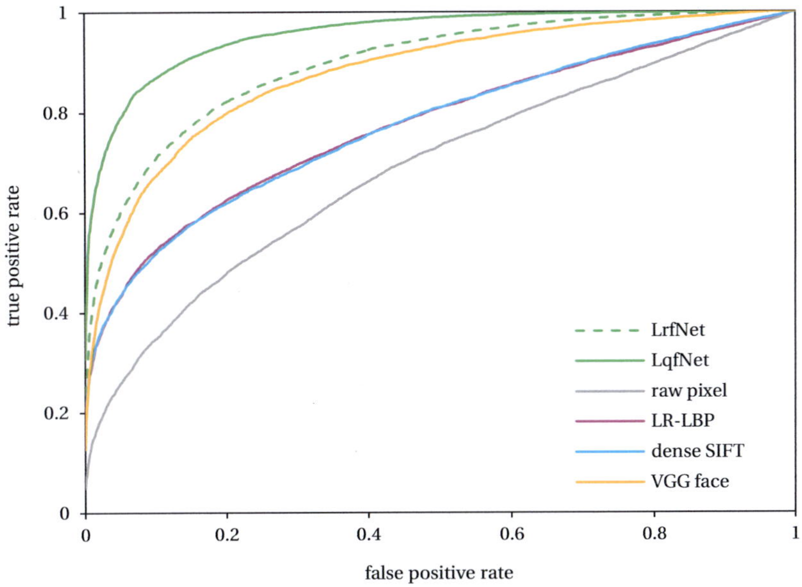

Figure 6.10: ROC-curves on IOSB-SURV test set. Only classical LrfNet and LqfNet are shown.

- The minset track descriptor is slow and methods based on it are consequently inappropriate for retrieval tasks. The proposed inverted index strategy combined with the LR-LBP face image descriptor yields comparable performance while requiring only a fraction of the query time for the higher-quality ChokePoint data. It appears to suffer more from the low image quality in IOSB-SURV than the further sequence descriptors although it is an unsupervised strategy.
- Further speedup is achieved by the supervised strategy because of the lower dimensional LrfNet and LqfNet face image descriptors which can also be efficiently aggregated along the face sequence by LMM.
- While the best methods perform excellently for the ChokePoint dataset and offer a high practical usability in this case, the additional in-the-wild challenges in the IOSB-SURV data lead to more mixed results. The top *map* of 0.593, means that most queries offer good results leading to a satisfactory overall usability, but some cases remain where a

human operator would judge the query result as disappointing. The next section will present a few examples for better interpretation of these numbers.

Altogether, the proposed unsupervised inverted index strategy improves the query time significantly compared to the baseline unsupervised strategies while preserving their performance level at least in the high-quality case. The proposed supervised strategy further improves the retrieval capabilities significantly, both with respect to a better matching performance as well as faster face search.

Table 6.12: Verification results on test datasets.

	ChokePoint		**IOSB-SURV**	
	acc	*std*	*acc*	*std*
raw pixel + minset	0.656	0.073	0.636	0.030
dense SIFT + minset	0.734	0.053	0.711	0.025
LR-LBP + minset	0.704	0.059	0.715	0.022
VGG-Face + *LMM*	0.938	0.041	0.795	0.023
LrfNet classical + *LMM*	0.947	0.022	0.814	0.014
LrfNet residual + *LMM*	0.932	0.045	0.816	0.020
LrfNet inception + *LMM*	**0.974**	**0.020**	0.791	0.028
LqfNet classical + *LMM*	0.967	0.028	**0.883**	**0.019**
LqfNet residual + *LMM*	0.952	0.030	0.830	0.020
LqfNet inception + *LMM*	0.965	0.035	0.815	0.019

Table 6.13: Retrieval results on test datasets.

	ChokePoint		**IOSB-SURV**	
	map	t_q in s	*map*	t_q in s
raw pixel + minset	0.264	1.51	0.182	7.57
dense SIFT + minset	0.445	1.74	0.314	6.91
LR-LBP + minset	0.405	3.61	0.292	10.47
LR-LBP + *loc. inv. index*	0.410	0.04	0.154	0.06
VGG-Face + *LMM*	0.894	0.02	0.428	0.05
LrfNet classical + *LMM*	0.888	**0.01**	0.419	**0.03**
LrfNet residual + *LMM*	0.895	**0.01**	0.424	**0.03**
LrfNet inception + *LMM*	0.953	**0.01**	0.451	**0.03**
LqfNet classical + *LMM*	**0.954**	**0.01**	**0.593**	**0.03**
LqfNet residual + *LMM*	0.914	**0.01**	0.419	**0.03**
LqfNet inception + *LMM*	0.931	**0.01**	0.336	**0.03**

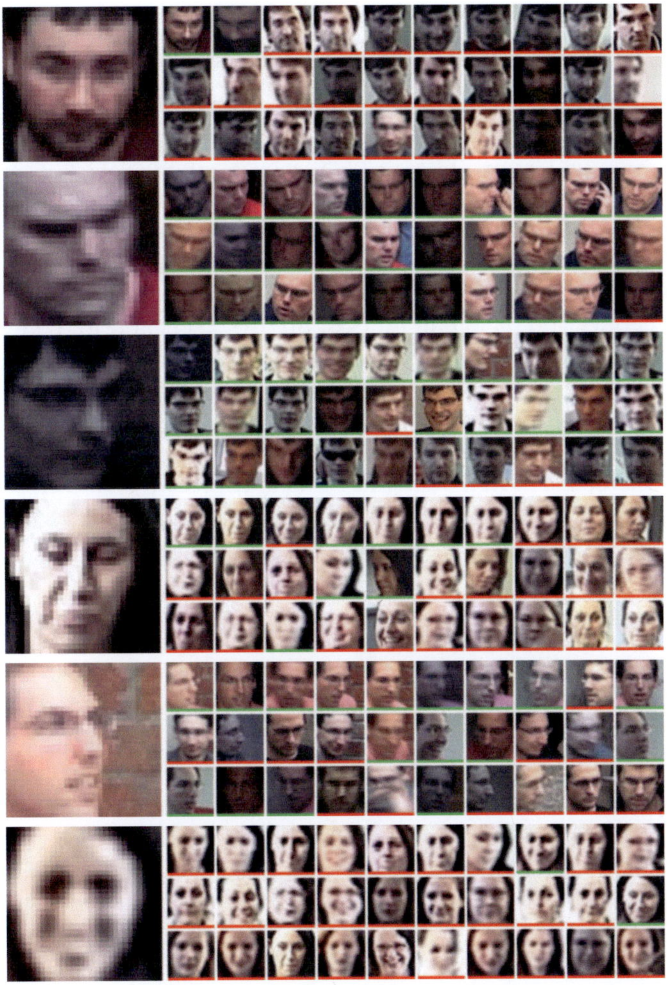

$ap = 1.0$
$Re(30) = 1.0$

$ap = 0.78$
$Re(30) = 0.36$

$ap = 0.64$
$Re(30) = 0.52$

$ap = 0.50$
$Re(30) = 0.60$

$ap = 0.40$
$Re(30) = 0.13$

$ap = 0.11$
$Re(30) = 1.0$

Figure 6.11: Top 30 search results for each query face sequence depicted on the left. All correct matches are indicated in green and achieved average precision and recall are denoted for each query individually.

6.4.2 Exemplary High-Quality Queries and Qualitative Results

To visualize the capabilities of the proposed CNN-based strategy, a few exemplary query results for the IOSB-SURV dataset are presented in figure 6.11. Depicted are the center frames of the respective face sequence. Overall, a good robustness to head pose, image quality and inaccurate face alignment is observed. The last aspect is important because alignment methods tend to degrade with decreasing image quality [Her15e]. If wrong matches are included in the top search results, they show mostly highly similar faces with matching gender and hair color (dark or bright). Especially for really low data quality when discriminative face features are sparse, the system appears to rely on such appearance attributes. In case of the last example, it is even hard for a human to correctly identify the matches and the proposed method ranked both occurrences within the top 20 out of the more than 5,000 samples. Even though this result is impressive, it indicates together with the example above that below average results can be expected for queries with extreme pose or extreme illumination.

Figure 6.12: Top 30 search results for querying with the high-quality mugshot-like face images depicted on the left. Correct matches are indicated in green and average precision and recall are denoted for each query individually.

Despite not explicitly designed for image-to-video comparison, a few according tests are performed to underline the capabilities of the proposed system. Instead of video samples, high-quality face images taken from profile images serve as query samples. Because high-quality images are only available for a subset of all persons in the IOSB-SURV dataset, no systematic evaluation is possible in this case and only selected results are shown in figure 6.12. Again, the image quality differences are handled robustly. In addition, results are still good in case of the partial face occlusions caused by glasses in the second case.

Table 6.14: Benefit of contributions on test datasets. The significance indicator based on p according to the randomization test is given in relation to the line above. LA denotes location augmentation and PA denotes pose augmentation.

image descriptor	sequence descriptor	presented in section	IOSB-SURV		
			map	$p < 0.05$	t_q in s
$\text{LBP}_{8,1}^{u2}$ + LA	inv. index	baseline	0.045		**0.04**
LR-LBP + LA	inv. index	4.1.1	0.074	✓	0.05
LR-LBP	local inv. index	5.2.3	0.148	✓	0.05
LR-LBP + PA	local inv. index	4.1.3	**0.155**	✓	0.05
VGG-Face	MSM	baseline	0.396	✓	0.19
LrfNet classical (contrastive)	MSM	4.2.1	0.142		0.11
LrfNet classical (max-margin)	MSM	4.2.3	0.410	✓	0.11
LqfNet classical	MSM	4.2.2	0.570	✓	0.11
LqfNet classical	LMM	5.3	**0.593**	✓	**0.04**

6.4.3 Benefit of Contributions

The different contributions of this thesis and their respective effect on the results in the target scenario are presented compactly in table 6.14. It can be clearly seen that all of them are required to improve the results to the final level. The major improvements originate from the local inverted index strategy, the max-margin loss and the center-based sequence descriptor. All three improve at least the retrieval performance or the search duration while not deteriorating the other. By this, their benefit is proven to be more than a mere trade-off between these opposing goals. Altogether, the contributions for the unsupervised strategy boost the performance significantly. Nevertheless, the generalization capabilities of the CNN are proven to be excellent, leading to a significantly better overall performance than the unsupervised local inverted index strategy. The large domain gap between the training data and the target scenario is easily compensated.

6.4.4 Network Insights

The reasons for the effectiveness of monolithic CNNs are more difficult to track down than for conventional image processing strategies which typically consist of several well understood small modules. Two strategies to inspect and gain insights into a trained CNN will be followed here. This allows to judge whether reasonable concepts were learned and to identify potential shortcomings which may indicate room for improvements. First, properties of the target space, and second, the learned convolution filters will be analyzed.

Descriptor Space

To get insights what the deep network learned, the target space of the classical LqfNet is analyzed. Visual inspection of the high-dimensional space is performed by t-Distributed Stochastic Neighbor Embedding (t-SNE) [Maa08] into two dimensional space. The t-SNE method is an unsupervised non-linear dimension reduction technique which is known to work well for projecting high-dimensional data to two or three dimensions for visualization. The distribution of face sequence descriptors is plotted for all 45 identities in the IOSB-SURV dataset who gave their consent to publish their images. Two different sequence properties are highlighted. First, equal coloring of sequences from the same identity in figure 6.13 indicates that the sequences of each identity are clustered together closely in the target space as desired. The second observation is that certain soft biometric attributes are also clustered together. Most notably, the sequences are nearly perfectly separable with respect to gender, as shown in figure 6.14, although the training process never saw gender annotations. This intrinsic face property was automatically discovered in the training process as being discriminative and helpful for face recognition. This suggests that future improvements might be possible by explicitly providing identity correlated face attributes, such as the age, in the training process to support target space structuring.

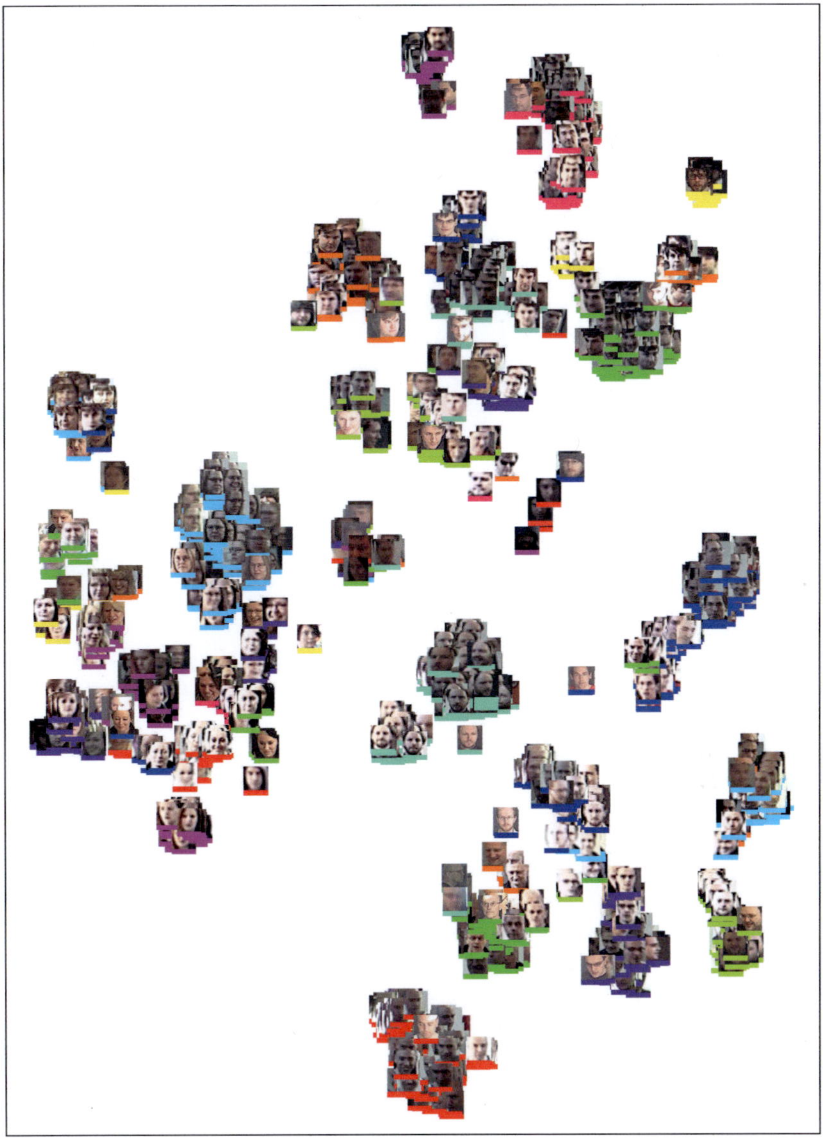

Figure 6.13: Visualization of target space by 2D t-SNE mapping for classical LqfNet face track descriptors for 45 IOSB-SURV identities. Each face image is the center frame of a sequence. Colors indicate identity.

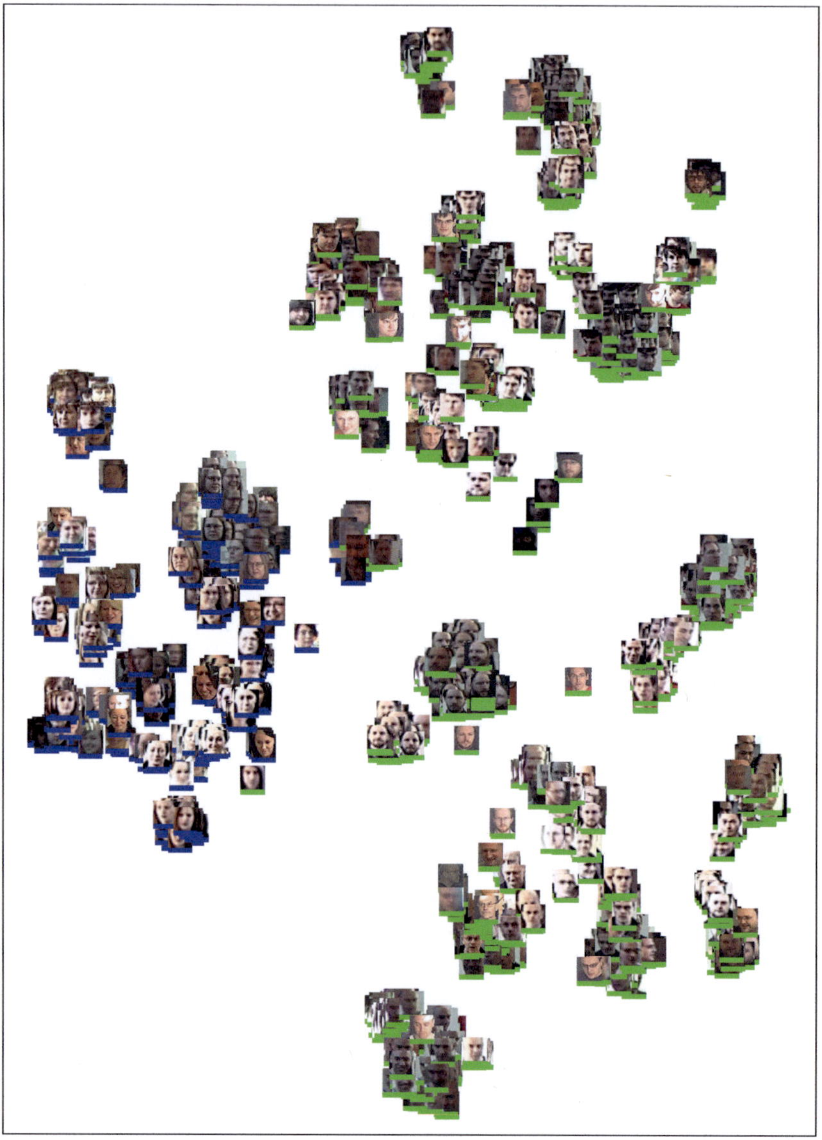

Figure 6.14: Visualization of target space by 2D t-SNE mapping for classical LqfNet face track descriptors for 45 IOSB-SURV identities. Each face image is the center frame of a sequence. Colors indicate gender.

Network Filter Responses

An intuitive way to manually inspect the processing strategy of a CNN is to visualize the image patches causing the highest filter responses as suggested in [Zei14]. To get a better intuition about typical filters, the classical LqfNet is compared with the general image categorization VGG-16 network [Sim15] and the HR face recognition VGG-Face network [Par15].

Figure 6.15: Image patches resulting in the highest responses of the learned filters [Zei14]. Depicted are the 9 highest response image patches for each filter of the first convolutional layer. Filters are loosely grouped by similarity for easier interpretation.

Because the VGG-Face network is trained with a transfer-learning strategy based on the general purpose VGG-16 network, potential face domain specific effects which cause filters to get adapted become obvious. For each filter in the first convolutional layer, the 9 image patches generating the highest response are depicted in figure 6.15. For better interpretation, the original colored patches are depicted also for the LqfNet even though it operates on gray scale input.

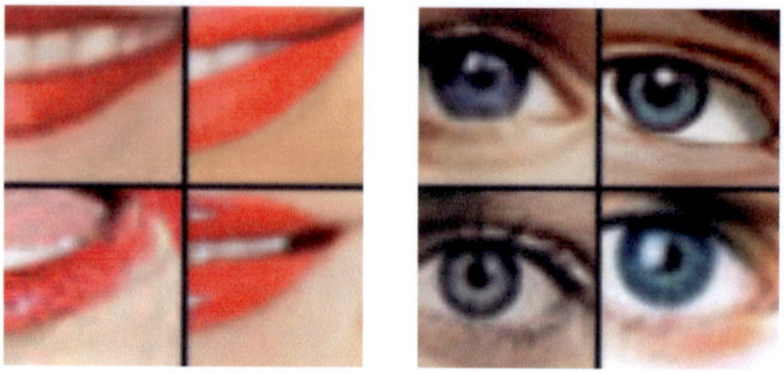

Figure 6.16: Face regions with high responses of the VGG-Face network color sensitive filters.

Several relevant aspects can be noted:

- While the general purpose VGG-16 includes a large variety of filters responding to 6 basic colors, edges and dots, the VGG-Face network shows a more distinct behavior. Only two colors, red and cyan, appear to be useful for face recognition. Thus, color information can be considered much less useful for the face recognition domain.
- Further analysis shows that the color filters in VGG-Face fire mainly on two face attributes: lips with intense red lipstick and bright blue eyes (figure 6.16). This yields another explanation why color information had no positive influence in case of the LqfNet. First, the eyes are too small in LR images to detect the eye color reliably. Second, intense lipstick is often worn by celebrities in photo shootings. Such images served for the VGG-Face training process, but are unrepresentative for the less common everyday use of lipstick. In addition, it is often worn inconsistently thus being no reliable indicator for person identity.
- Dot structures are lost in favor of more edge filters in course of fine-tuning VGG-16 to VGG-Face.
- The LqfNet again includes filters responding to dot structures as well as a more fine-grained selection of edge filters, indicating that the higher number of filters is necessary to gather all relevant information.

Overall, the network analysis indicates a well-trained LqfNet, offers further explanations for previous findings in case of color information and indicates directions for future research with face attributes.

6.4.5 Target Domain Test Summary

Most importantly, the target domain tests showed that the proposed data augmentation is beneficial for low-quality data. This is why the supervised CNN-based strategy achieved excellent search results despite the large domain gap to the training data. In comparison, the unsupervised method allowed similarly fast face search but achieved a significantly lower performance which is negatively affected by the low-quality domain. In both cases, it is shown that all respective contributions improve the results towards the final level. The search results of the supervised strategy are beneficial for a human operator as is shown with representative examples.

7 Conclusions and Outlook

7.1 Conclusions

Two strategies for large-scale face retrieval in low-quality video data are proposed in this thesis and both allow a fast face search within milliseconds in large amounts of indexed video data. The focus lies on large-scale low-quality surveillance video footage and most contributions in this thesis address either the required fast search or the low data quality. Regarding the recognition performance, the supervised strategy based on a CNN face image descriptor is proven to be superior to the unsupervised strategy based on LBPs and inverted indices, despite the domain gap between the high-quality public training datasets and the low-quality surveillance domain.

While the unsupervised LBP descriptor has no risk of overfitting to the high-quality domain, it is less specialized to recognizing faces than the supervised CNN descriptor. A multi-scale histogram fusion is applied to improve the LBP descriptor for LR faces which have a size down to 25×25 pixels in the collected surveillance data. The combination with the local inverted index strategy to aggregate face image descriptors along a sequence incorporates an unsupervised descriptor adaptation to the face domain. The proposed local indices significantly improve the matching performance compared with a single global index but are unable to catch up with the performance of the supervised strategy.

The proposed training data augmentation by low-quality samples proves to be an efficient way to close the domain gap for the supervised CNN face image descriptor while involving no additional cost at runtime. In this way, successful face retrieval is performed on the surveillance video data, which includes significant motion blur, noise and compression artifacts. The systematic CNN architecture optimization is essential for achieving the high performance because the LR face images require the use of an architecture that differs from widespread HR networks. In comparison, the result of the optimization is a shallower, but wider network architecture. A fast face search is achieved by fusing the face image descriptors into a 128-dimensional face sequence descriptor which is efficiently compared by Euclidean distance. The motivation for the center-based fusion is given by the enforced target space compactness of the proposed max-margin loss function. To assess both methods' capabilities regarding LR conditions, validation experiments are performed with rescaled face images starting from a face size of 8×8 pixels up to 40×40 pixels. As expected, the performance increases with the resolution, but improvements beyond 28×28 pixels tend to be smaller than below.

Compared with the state-of-the-art VGG-Face descriptor, the proposed LqfNet descriptor improves the retrieval performance significantly on low-quality surveillance data while reducing the search duration by a factor of 2 and the index database size by a factor of 20. Example queries indicated that the search results can be considered beneficial for a human operator and support the forensic analysis of large-scale video data in the context of investigations. In addition, besides the targeted low-quality samples, high-quality query samples lead also to comparable search results in the low-quality video data proving cross-domain suitability. The results on the LR version of the YTF dataset showed that the proposed LR method is on par with the human HR face recognition capabilities in this case.

7.2 Outlook

Currently, automatic face recognition surpasses human capabilities in more and more scenarios with humans being already beaten on the most well-known scientific face datasets LFW [Kum09, Lu15], YTF [BR14, Sch15b] and IARPA Janus Benchmark-A (IJB-A) [Bla16, Lu17]. While surpassing the human face recognition capability is a tempting goal, some practical applications demand substantially better performance, especially when thinking of web-scale face search. Several future research directions are identified to further improve the face retrieval methods in this direction.

1. Both proposed strategies would allow a **re-ranking** based on user relevance feedback [Bäu10]. In the easiest case, search results indicated as correct samples by the user can be added to the query to improve the refined results. This would conceptually be possible in both systems. More elaborate strategies, which may, for example, also include negative feedback, offer more space for performance progresses but tend to demand more user involvement thus reducing usability.
2. The results showed that the unsupervised strategy lacks in performance, which suggests to focus future effort on core improvements of the CNN system. Promising directions include:
   - An **all-in-one network**. Currently, state-of-the-art face detection, alignment and recognition are usually all performed by CNNs but separately. In the sense of a complete end-to-end learning, it is desirable to merge all networks together in a unified solution. This would reduce the hassle of manually optimizing the recognition strategy to the detector and alignment, and vice-versa. The respective adaptation would be data-driven. Recently, an all-in-one network including the mentioned components and additionally age and emotion estimation was presented [Ran16]. However, their face detection approach is rather inefficient with a reported processing time of 3.5s per image, making this solution unsuitable for large-scale processing.
   - **Incorporating face attributes**. Inspection of the target space showed a high discriminative capability with regard to the gender. Explicit usage of such attribute information as, for example, gender, age, facial hair or hair style, on network training might help to further structure the target space and help the network identify useful features. The drawback is the rather extensively annotated data which is required for this concept.
   - **Better loss functions**. An increasingly studied topic are loss functions for network training [Din16b, Wen16] which try to enforce a better intra-class compactness of the descriptor in the target space. In theory, this results in better separability of identities by less outliers causing errors.

- **Additional relevant training data.** Because CNNs are largely data-driven, increasing the training data size leads to improvements as long as additional data is relevant. In the scope of this thesis, a large-scale face video surveillance dataset with at least a 5 or 6 digit number of training sequences can be expected to significantly improve the results. The proposed data augmentation made a huge step in exploiting this potential, but using actual in-the-wild data is expected to yield even better results.

3. Regarding the practical applicability with respect to runtime, the most significant bottlenecks of the supervised system are the descriptor comparison and the CNN inference. For CNN inference, it was shown that weight and input data depth can be quantized, for example, to an 8-bit fixed float instead of a 32-bit floating point format without major loss in performance [Han15, Lin16]. In addition to data depth modifications, network pruning [Han15] is another promising way to reduce the inference duration and size of a network. Elimination of unused or non-contributing network parts saves the respective computations and leads to sparser networks. For descriptor comparison, data binarization [Par14] can increase the comparison speed because Euclidean distance breaks down into a sum and logical AND operations which are highly efficient in modern processor instruction sets. Another binarization approach would be to map the $\mathbb{R}^d$ CNN face sequence descriptors to a $\{0,1\}^m$ binary representation in a way that inverted index search becomes possible [Don15b].

When improving a retrieval system, one has to keep in mind both often competing goals: a high performance and a low search duration. While most of the suggestions aim to optimize only one goal, better loss functions are the best option to push both goals by enforcing a more discriminative target space which has less dimensions than the proposed solution.

Bibliography

[Agi06] AGICHTEIN, Eugene; BRILL, Eric and DUMAIS, Susan: Improving web search ranking by incorporating user behavior information, in: *Conference on Research and Development in Information Retrieval*, ACM (2006), pp. 19–26

[Aho04] AHONEN, Timo; HADID, Abdenour and PIETIKÄINEN, Matti: Face Recognition With Local Binary Patterns, in: *European Conference on Computer Vision*, Springer (2004), pp. 469–481

[Aho06] AHONEN, Timo; HADID, Abdenour and PIETIKAINEN, Matti: Face Description with Local Binary Patterns: Application to Face Recognition. *IEEE Transactions on Pattern Analysis and Machine Intelligence* (2006), vol. 28(12): pp. 2037–2041

[Alb08] ALBIOL, Alberto; MONZO, David; MARTIN, Antoine; SASTRE, Jorge and ALBIOL, Antonio: Face recognition using HOG–EBGM. *Pattern Recognition Letters* (2008), vol. 29(10): pp. 1537–1543

[Ara06b] ARANDJELOVIĆ, O. and CIPOLLA, R.: Face Recognition from Video Using the Generic Shape-illumination Manifold, in: *European Conference on Computer Vision*, Springer (2006), pp. 27–40

[Ara09b] ARANDJELOVIĆ, O. and CIPOLLA, R.: A pose-wise linear illumination manifold model for face recognition using video. *Computer Vision and Image Understanding* (2009), vol. 113(1): pp. 113–125

[Ara12d] ARANDJELOVIC, Relja and ZISSERMAN, Andrew: Three things everyone should know to improve object retrieval, in: *Conference on Computer Vision and Pattern Recognition*, IEEE (2012), pp. 2911–2918

[Bal10] BALL, Roger; SHU, Chang; XI, Pengcheng; RIOUX, Marc; LUXIMON, Yan and MOLENBROEK, Johan: A comparison between Chinese and Caucasian head shapes. *Applied Ergonomics* (2010), vol. 41(6): pp. 832–839

[Ban16] BANSAL, Ankan; CASTILLO, Carlos; RANJAN, Rajeev and CHELLAPPA, Rama: UMDFaces: An Annotated Face Dataset for Training Deep Networks. *arXiv preprint arXiv:1611.01484* (2016)

[Bar12] BARR, Jeremiah R; BOWYER, Kevin W; FLYNN, Patrick J and BISWAS, Soma: Face recognition from video: A review. *International Journal of Pattern Recognition and Artificial Intelligence* (2012), vol. 26(05)

[Bäu10] BÄUML, M.; BERNARDIN, K.; FISCHER, M.; EKENEL, H.K. and STIEFELHAGEN, R.: Multi-pose face recognition for person retrieval in camera networks, in: *International Conference on Advanced Video and Signal-Based Surveillance*, IEEE (2010)

[Bäu13] BÄUML, Martin; TAPASWI, Makarand and STIEFELHAGEN, Rainer: Semi-supervised learning with constraints for person identification in multimedia data, in: *Conference on Computer Vision and Pattern Recognition*, IEEE (2013), pp. 3602–3609

[Bäu14] BÄUML, Martin; TAPASWI, Makarand and STIEFELHAGEN, Rainer: A time pooled track kernel for person identification, in: *International Conference on Advanced Video and Signal-Based Surveillance*, IEEE (2014), pp. 7–12

[Bei97] BEIS, Jeffrey S and LOWE, David G: Shape indexing using approximate nearest-neighbour search in high-dimensional spaces, in: *Conference on Computer Vision and Pattern Recognition*, IEEE (1997), pp. 1000–1006

[Bel97] BELHUMEUR, P.N.; HESPANHA, J.P. and KRIEGMAN, D.J.: Eigenfaces vs. Fisherfaces: Recognition Using Class Specific Linear Projection. *IEEE Transactions on Pattern Analysis and Machine Intelligence* (1997), vol. 19(7): pp. 711–720

[Ber12] BERG, Thomas and BELHUMEUR, Peter N: Tom-vs-Pete Classifiers and Identity-Preserving Alignment for Face Verification., in: *British Machine Vision Conference* (2012)

[Bev13] BEVERIDGE, J Ross; PHILLIPS, P Jonathon; BOLME, David S; DRAPER, Bruce A; GIVENS, Geof H; LUI, Yui Man; TELI, Mohammad Nayeem; ZHANG, Hao; SCRUGGS, W Todd; BOWYER, Kevin W ET AL.: The challenge of face recognition from digital point-and-shoot cameras, in: *International Conference on Biometrics: Theory, Applications and Systems*, IEEE (2013), pp. 1–8

[Bla01] BLACKBURN, Duane Michael; PHILLIPS, P Jonathon and BONE, Mike: *Facial recognition vendor test 2000 evaluation report*, US Department of Defense (2001)

[Bla16] BLANTON, Austin; ALLEN, Kristen C; MILLER, Timothy; KALKA, Nathan D and JAIN, Anil K: A Comparison of Human and Automated Face Verification Accuracy on Unconstrained Image Sets, in: *Conference on Computer Vision and Pattern Recognition Workshops*, IEEE (2016), pp. 161–168

[Bod17] BODLA, Navaneeth; ZHENG, Jingxiao; XU, Hongyu; CHEN, Jun-Cheng; CASTILLO, Carlos and CHELLAPPA, Rama: Deep Heterogeneous Feature Fusion for Template-Based Face Recognition, in: *Winter Conference on Applications of Computer Vision*, IEEE (2017)

[Bol05] BOLLE, Ruud M; CONNELL, Jonathan H; PANKANTI, Sharath; RATHA, Nalini K and SENIOR, Andrew W: The relation between the ROC curve and the CMC, in: *Workshop on Automatic Identification Advanced Technologies* (2005)

[Bou17] BOULT, Terrance E.; GÜNTHER, Manuel and DHAMIJA, Akshay Raj: UnConstrained College Students (UCCS) Dataset (2017), URL http://vast.uccs.edu/Opensetface/

[BR14] BEST-ROWDEN, Lacey; BISHT, Shiwani; KLONTZ, Joshua C and JAIN, Anil K: Unconstrained face recognition: Establishing baseline human performance via crowdsourcing, in: *International Joint Conference on Biometrics*, IEEE (2014), pp. 1–8

[Bro94] BROMLEY, Jane; GUYON, Isabelle; LECUN, Yann; SÄCKINGER, Eduard and SHAH, Roopak: Signature verification using a" siamese" time delay neural network, in: *Advances in Neural Information Processing Systems* (1994), pp. 737–744

[Bur99] BURTON, A Mike; WILSON, Stephen; COWAN, Michelle and BRUCE, Vicki: Face recognition in poor-quality video: Evidence from security surveillance. *Psychological Science* (1999), vol. 10(3): pp. 243–248

[Cev10] CEVIKALP, H. and TRIGGS, B.: Face recognition based on image sets, in: *Conference on Computer Vision and Pattern Recognition*, IEEE (2010)

[Cha17] CHANG, Le and TSAO, Doris Y: The Code for Facial Identity in the Primate Brain. *Cell* (2017), vol. 169(6): pp. 1013–1028

[Che95] CHELLAPPA, Rama; WILSON, Charles L and SIROHEY, Saad: Human and machine recognition of faces: A survey. *Proceedings of the IEEE* (1995), vol. 83(5): pp. 705–741

[Che11b] CHEN, Shaokang; MAU, Sandra; HARANDI, Mehrtash T.; SANDERSON, Conrad; BIGDELI, Abbas and LOVELL, Brian C.: Face Recognition from Still Images to Video Sequences: A Local-feature-based Framework. *EURASIP Journal on Image and Video Processing* (2011)

[Che13a] CHEN, B; CHEN, Y; KUO, Y and HSU, W: Scalable face image retrieval using attribute-enhanced sparse codewords. *Transactions on Multimedia* (2013), vol. 15(5): pp. 1163–1173

[Che16] CHEN, Jun-Cheng; PATEL, Vishal M and CHELLAPPA, Rama: Unconstrained face verification using deep cnn features, in: *Applications of Computer Vision (WACV), 2016 IEEE Winter Conference on*, IEEE (2016), pp. 1–9

[Cho05] CHOPRA, Sumit; HADSELL, Raia and LECUN, Yann: Learning a similarity metric discriminatively, with application to face verification, in: *Conference on Computer Vision and Pattern Recognition*, vol. 1, IEEE (2005), pp. 539–546

[Den09] DENG, Jia; DONG, Wei; SOCHER, Richard; LI, Li-Jia; LI, Kai and FEI-FEI, Li: Imagenet: A large-scale hierarchical image database, in: *Conference on Computer Vision and Pattern Recognition*, IEEE (2009), pp. 248–255

[Din15] DING, Sihao; LI, Ying; ZHU, Junda; ZHENG, Yuan F and XUAN, Dong: Sequential sample consensus: A robust algorithm for video-based face recognition. *IEEE Transactions on Circuits and Systems for Video Technology* (2015), vol. 25(10): pp. 1586–1598

[Din16a] DING, Changxing and TAO, Dacheng: A comprehensive survey on pose-invariant face recognition. *ACM Transactions on Intelligent Systems and Technology* (2016), vol. 7(3): p. 37

[Din16b] DING, Changxing and TAO, Dacheng: Trunk-Branch Ensemble Convolutional Neural Networks for Video-based Face Recognition. *arXiv preprint arXiv:1607.05427* (2016)

[DM14] DE MARSICO, M.: *Face Recognition in Adverse Conditions*, Advances in Computational Intelligence and Robotics:, IGI Global (2014)

[Don15b] DONALDSON, Roger; GUPTA, Arijit; PLAN, Yaniv and REIMER, Thomas: Random mappings designed for commercial search engines. *arXiv preprint arXiv:1507.05929* (2015)

[Dud01] DUDA, R.O.; HART, P.E. and STORK, D.G.: *Pattern Classification*, Wiley, second edition edn. (2001)

[Duf08] DUFFNER, Stefan: *Face image analysis with convolutional neural networks*, Ph.D. thesis, University of Freiburg, Germany (2008)

[Eke06] EKENEL, Hazim Kemal and STIEFELHAGEN, Rainer: Analysis of local appearance-based face recognition: Effects of feature selection and feature normalization, in: *Conference on Computer Vision and Pattern Recognition*, IEEE (2006), pp. 34–34

[Eve06] EVERINGHAM, M.; SIVIC, J. and ZISSERMAN, A.: Hello! My name is... Buffy–Automatic naming of characters in TV video, in: *British Machine Vision Conference* (2006)

[Far16] FAROKHI, Sajad; FLUSSER, Jan and SHEIKH, Usman Ullah: Near infrared face recognition: A literature survey. *Computer Science Review* (2016), vol. 21: pp. 1–17

[Fis12] FISCHER, Mika; EKENEL, Hazım Kemal and STIEFELHAGEN, Rainer: Analysis of partial least squares for pose-invariant face recognition, in: *International Conference on Biometrics: Theory, Applications and Systems*, IEEE (2012), pp. 331–338

[Fri77] FRIEDMAN, Jerome H; BENTLEY, Jon Louis and FINKEL, Raphael Ari: An algorithm for finding best matches in logarithmic expected time. *ACM Transactions on Mathematical Software (TOMS)* (1977), vol. 3(3): pp. 209–226

[Fro04] FROBA, Bernhard and ERNST, Andreas: Face detection with the modified census transform, in: *International Conference on Automatic Face and Gesture Recognition*, IEEE (2004), pp. 91–96

[Fuk05] FUKUI, K. and YAMAGUCHI, O.: Face Recognition Using Multiviewpoint Patterns for Robot Vision. *Robotics Research* (2005): pp. 192–201

[Gar02] GARCIA, Christophe and DELAKIS, Manolis: A neural architecture for fast and robust face detection, in: *International Conference on Pattern Recognition*, vol. 2, IEEE (2002), pp. 44–47

[Gar04] GARCIA, Christophe and DELAKIS, Manolis: Convolutional face finder: A neural architecture for fast and robust face detection. *IEEE Transactions on Pattern Analysis and Machine Intelligence* (2004), vol. 26(11): pp. 1408–1423

[Geo00] GEORGHIADES, A.S.; BELHUMEUR, P.N. and KRIEGMAN, D.J.: From Few To Many: Generative Models For Recognition Under Variable Pose And Illumination, in: *International Conference on Automatic Face and Gesture Recognition*, IEEE (2000), pp. 277–284

[Gha15] GHALEB, Esam; TAPASWI, Makarand; AL-HALAH, Ziad; EKENEL, Hazim Kemal and STIEFELHAGEN, Rainer: Accio: a data set for face track retrieval in movies across age, in: *ACM International Conference on Multimedia Retrieval*, ACM (2015), pp. 455–458

[Glo10] GLOROT, Xavier and BENGIO, Yoshua: Understanding the difficulty of training deep feedforward neural networks., in: *Aistats*, vol. 9 (2010), pp. 249–256

[Goh05] GOH, R.; LIU, L.; LIU, X. and CHEN, T.: The CMU Face In Action (FIA) Database. *Analysis and Modelling of Faces and Gestures* (2005): pp. 255–263

[Gor05] GORODNICHY, Dmitry O: Video-based framework for face recognition in video, in: *Canadian Conference on Computer and Robot Vision*, IEEE (2005), pp. 330–338

[Grg11] GRGIC, Mislav; DELAC, Kresimir and GRGIC, Sonja: SCface–surveillance cameras face database. *Multimedia tools and applications* (2011), vol. 51(3): pp. 863–879

[Gro01] GROSS, Ralph and SHI, Jianbo: The CMU motion of body (MoBo) database (2001)

[Gro10a] GROSS, R.; MATTHEWS, I.; COHN, J.; KANADE, T. and BAKER, S.: Multi-PIE. *Image and Vision Computing* (2010), vol. 28(5): pp. 807–813

[Gro10b] GROTHER, Patrick J; QUINN, George W and PHILLIPS, P Jonathon: Report on the evaluation of 2D still-image face recognition algorithms. *NIST interagency report* (2010), vol. 7709: p. 106

[Gro13] GROTHER, Patrick and NGAN, Mei: Face recognition vendor test (frvt)-performance of face identification algorithms. nist interagency report 8009, Tech. Rep., Tech. rep., NIST (May 2014). 340 (2013)

[Guo16] GUO, Yandong; ZHANG, Lei; HU, Yuxiao; HE, Xiaodong and GAO, Jianfeng: MS-Celeb-1M: Challenge of Recognizing One Million Celebrities in the Real World, in: *Imaging and Multimedia Analytics in a Web and Mobile World* (2016)

[Had04] HADID, Abdenour and PIETIKAINEN, M: From still image to video-based face recognition: an experimental analysis, in: *International Conference on Automatic Face and Gesture Recognition*, IEEE (2004), pp. 813–818

[Had06] HADSELL, Raia; CHOPRA, Sumit and LECUN, Yann: Dimensionality reduction by learning an invariant mapping, in: *Conference on Computer Vision and Pattern Recognition*, vol. 2, IEEE (2006), pp. 1735–1742

[Had09c] HADID, A. and PIETIKÄINEN, M.: Manifold learning for video-to-video face recognition. *Biometric ID Management and Multimodal Communication* (2009): pp. 9–16

[Han15] HAN, Song; MAO, Huizi and DALLY, William J: Deep compression: Compressing deep neural networks with pruning, trained quantization and huffman coding. *arXiv preprint arXiv:1510.00149* (2015)

[He15a] HE, Kaiming; ZHANG, Xiangyu; REN, Shaoqing and SUN, Jian: Deep Residual Learning for Image Recognition. *arXiv preprint arXiv:1512.03385* (2015)

[He15b] HE, Kaiming; ZHANG, Xiangyu; REN, Shaoqing and SUN, Jian: Delving deep into rectifiers: Surpassing human-level performance on imagenet classification, in: *International Conference on Computer Vision*, IEEE (2015), pp. 1026–1034

[He16] HE, Kaiming; ZHANG, Xiangyu; REN, Shaoqing and SUN, Jian: Identity mappings in deep residual networks. *arXiv preprint arXiv:1603.05027* (2016)

[Hei03] HEISELE, Bernd; HO, Purdy; WU, Jane and POGGIO, Tomaso: Face recognition: component-based versus global approaches. *Computer Vision and Image Understanding* (2003), vol. 91(1): pp. 6–21

[Hu14] HU, Junlin; LU, Jiwen and TAN, Yap-Peng: Discriminative deep metric learning for face verification in the wild, in: *Conference on Computer Vision and Pattern Recognition* (2014)

[Hua07] HUANG, Gary B.; RAMESH, Manu; BERG, Tamara and LEARNED-MILLER, Erik: Labeled Faces in the Wild: A Database for Studying Face Recognition in Unconstrained Environments, Tech. Rep. 07-49, University of Massachusetts, Amherst (2007)

[Hua11] HUANG, C.; ZHU, S. and YU, K.: Large Scale Strongly Supervised Ensemble Metric Learning, with Applications to Face Verification and Retrieval. *NEC Technical Report* (2011)

[HY08] HENNINGS-YEOMANS, Pablo H; BAKER, Simon and KUMAR, BVK Vijaya: Simultaneous super-resolution and feature extraction for recognition of low-resolution faces, in: *Conference on Computer Vision and Pattern Recognition*, IEEE (2008), pp. 1–8

[Iof15] IOFFE, Sergey and SZEGEDY, Christian: Batch normalization: Accelerating deep network training by reducing internal covariate shift, in: *International Conference on Machine Learning* (2015)

[Jab10] JABID, Taskeed; KABIR, Md Hasanul and CHAE, Oksam: Local directional pattern (LDP) for face recognition, in: *Consumer Electronics* (2010), pp. 329–330

[Jaf09] JAFRI, Rabia and ARABNIA, Hamid R: A survey of face recognition techniques. *Jips* (2009), vol. 5(2): pp. 41–68

[Jai02] JAIN, Vidit and MUKHERJEE, Amitabha: The Indian Face Database (2002), URL http://vis-www.cs.umass.edu/~vidit/IndianFaceDatabase

[Jég08] JÉGOU, Hervé; DOUZE, Matthijs and SCHMID, Cordelia: Hamming embedding and weak geometry consistency for large scale image search, in: *European Conference on Computer Vision* (2008)

[Jen08] JENKINS, Rob and BURTON, AM: 100% Accuracy In Automatic Face Recognition. *Science* (2008), vol. 319(5862): pp. 435–435

[Jes01] JESORSKY, Oliver; KIRCHBERG, Klaus J and FRISCHHOLZ, Robert W: Robust face detection using the hausdorff distance, in: *International Conference on Audio-and Video-Based Biometric Person Authentication*, Springer (2001), pp. 90–95

[Jia14] JIA, Yangqing; SHELHAMER, Evan; DONAHUE, Jeff; KARAYEV, Sergey; LONG, Jonathan; GIRSHICK, Ross; GUADARRAMA, Sergio and DARRELL, Trevor: Caffe: Convolutional Architecture for Fast Feature Embedding. *arXiv preprint arXiv:1408.5093* (2014)

[Jia16] JIANG, Junjun; HU, Ruimin; WANG, Zhongyuan and CAI, Zhihua: CDMMA: Coupled discriminant multi-manifold analysis for matching low-resolution face images. *Signal Processing* (2016), vol. 124: pp. 162–172

[Kan77] KANADE, Takeo: *Computer recognition of human faces*, vol. 47 of *Interdisciplinary Systems Research*, Birkhäuser (1977)

[Kan02] KANUNGO, Tapas; MOUNT, David M; NETANYAHU, Nathan S; PIATKO, Christine D; SILVERMAN, Ruth and WU, Angela Y: An efficient k-means clustering algorithm: Analysis and implementation. *IEEE Transactions on Pattern Analysis and Machine Intelligence* (2002), vol. 24(7): pp. 881–892

[Kas08] KASINSKI, A.; FLOREK, A. and SCHMIDT, A.: The PUT Face Database. *Image Processing and Communications* (2008), vol. 13(3-4): pp. 59–64

[Kim08] KIM, M.; KUMAR, S.; PAVLOVIC, V. and ROWLEY, H.: Face tracking and recognition with visual constraints in real-world videos, in: *Conference on Computer Vision and Pattern Recognition*, IEEE (2008), pp. 1–8

[Kla15] KLARE, Brendan F; KLEIN, Ben; TABORSKY, Emma; BLANTON, Austin; CHENEY, Jordan; ALLEN, Kristen; GROTHER, Patrick; MAH, Alan and JAIN, Anil K: Pushing the frontiers of unconstrained face detection and recognition: IARPA Janus Benchmark A, in: *Conference on Computer Vision and Pattern Recognition*, IEEE (2015), pp. 1931–1939

[Kri12] KRIZHEVSKY, Alex; SUTSKEVER, Ilya and HINTON, Geoffrey E: Imagenet classification with deep convolutional neural networks, in: *Neural Information Processing Systems* (2012), pp. 1097–1105

[KS16] KEMELMACHER-SHLIZERMAN, Ira; SEITZ, Steven M; MILLER, Daniel and BROSSARD, Evan: The MegaFace Benchmark: 1 Million Faces for Recognition at Scale, in: *Conference on Computer Vision and Pattern Recognition*, IEEE (2016)

[Kum09] KUMAR, Neeraj; BERG, Alexander C; BELHUMEUR, Peter N and NAYAR, Shree K: Attribute and simile classifiers for face verification, in: *Conference on Computer Vision and Pattern Recognition*, IEEE (2009), pp. 365–372

[Kum11] KUMAR, Neeraj; BERG, Alexander; BELHUMEUR, Peter N and NAYAR, Shree: Describable visual attributes for face verification and image search. *IEEE Transactions on Pattern Analysis and Machine Intelligence* (2011), vol. 33(10): pp. 1962–1977

[Lai02] LAI, Jim ZC; LIAW, Yi-Ching and LO, Winston: Artifact reduction of JPEG coded images using mean-removed classified vector quantization. *Signal Processing* (2002), vol. 82(10): pp. 1375–1388

[Law97] LAWRENCE, Steve; GILES, C Lee; TSOI, Ah Chung and BACK, Andrew D: Face recognition: A convolutional neural-network approach. *IEEE Transactions on Neural Networks* (1997), vol. 8(1): pp. 98–113

[LC89] LE CUN, Yann; JACKEL, LD; BOSER, B; DENKER, JS; GRAF, HP; GUYON, I; HENDERSON, D; HOWARD, RE and HUBBARD, W: Handwritten digit recognition: Applications of neural network chips and automatic learning. *IEEE Communications Magazine* (1989), vol. 27(11): pp. 41–46

[LeC98] LECUN, Yann; BOTTOU, Léon; BENGIO, Yoshua and HAFFNER, Patrick: Gradient-based learning applied to document recognition. *Proceedings of the IEEE* (1998), vol. 86(11): pp. 2278–2324

[Lee03] LEE, K.C.; HO, J.; YANG, M.H. and KRIEGMAN, D.: Video-Based Face Recognition Using Probabilistic Appearance Manifolds, in: *Conference on Computer Vision and Pattern Recognition*, vol. 1, IEEE (2003), pp. 313–320

[Lee05] LEE, K.C.; HO, J.; YANG, M.H. and KRIEGMAN, D.: Visual Tracking and Recognition Using Probabilistic Appearance Manifolds. *Computer Vision and Image Understanding* (2005), vol. 99(3): pp. 303–331

[Li09] LI, Stan Z; SCHOUTEN, Ben and TISTARELLI, Massimo: Biometrics at a distance: issues, challenges, and prospects, in: *Handbook of Remote Biometrics*, Springer (2009), pp. 3–21

[Li11a] LI, A.; SHAN, S.; CHEN, X. and GAO, W.: Cross-pose face recognition based on partial least squares. *Pattern Recognition Letters* (2011)

[Li11c] LI, S.Z. and JAIN, A.K. (Editors): *Handbook of Face Recognition*, Springer, London, second edition edn. (2011)

[Li13] LI, Haoxiang; HUA, Gang; LIN, Zhe; BRANDT, Jonathan and YANG, Jianchao: Probabilistic elastic matching for pose variant face verification, in: *Conference on Computer Vision and Pattern Recognition,* IEEE (2013)

[Li14b] LI, Huibin; HUANG, Di; MORVAN, Jean-Marie; CHEN, Liming and WANG, Yunhong: Expression-Robust 3D Face Recognition via Weighted Sparse Representation of Multi-Scale and Multi-Component Local Normal Patterns. *Neurocomputing* (2014)

[Lia10] LIAO, Wen-Hung: Region description using extended local ternary patterns, in: *Pattern Recognition (ICPR), 2010 20th International Conference on,* IEEE (2010), pp. 1003–1006

[Lin16] LIN, Darryl; TALATHI, Sachin and ANNAPUREDDY, Sreekanth: Fixed point quantization of deep convolutional networks, in: *International Conference on Machine Learning* (2016)

[Liu14] LIU, Luoqi; ZHANG, Li; LIU, Hairong and YAN, Shuicheng: Toward large-population face identification in unconstrained videos. *IEEE Transactions on Circuits and Systems for Video Technology* (2014), vol. 24(11): pp. 1874–1884

[Liu16] LIU, Xin; KAN, Meina; WU, Wanglong; SHAN, Shiguang and CHEN, Xilin: VIPLFaceNet: An Open Source Deep Face Recognition SDK. *arXiv preprint arXiv:1609.03892* (2016)

[Lu15] LU, Chaochao and TANG, Xiaoou: Surpassing Human-Level Face Verification Performance on LFW with GaussianFace., in: *AAAI* (2015), pp. 3811–3819

[Lu17] LU, Boyu; ZHENG, Jingxiao; CHEN, Jun-Cheng and CHELLAPPA, Rama: Pose-Robust Face Verification by Exploiting Competing Tasks, in: *Winter Conference on Applications of Computer Vision,* IEEE (2017), pp. 1124–1132

[Lyo98] LYONS, Michael; AKAMATSU, Shigeru; KAMACHI, Miyuki and GYOBA, Jiro: Coding facial expressions with gabor wavelets, in: *Automatic Face and Gesture Recognition, 1998. Proceedings. Third IEEE International Conference on,* IEEE (1998), pp. 200–205

[Maa08] MAATEN, Laurens van der and HINTON, Geoffrey: Visualizing data using t-SNE. *Journal of Machine Learning Research* (2008), vol. 9(Nov): pp. 2579–2605

[Mar80] MARĈELJA, S: Mathematical description of the responses of simple cortical cells. *JOSA* (1980), vol. 70(11): pp. 1297–1300

[Mas16] MASI, Iacopo; TRAN, Anh Tuan; LEKSUT, Jatuporn Toy; HASSNER, Tal and MEDIONI, Gerard: Do we really need to collect millions of faces for effective face recognition? *arXiv preprint arXiv:1603.07057* (2016)

[McC03] MCCAHILL, Mike and NORRIS, Clive: Estimating the extent, sophistication and legality of CCTV in London. *CCTV* (2003): pp. 51–66

[McL15] MCLAUGHLIN, Niall; DEL RINCON, Jesus Martinez and MILLER, Paul: Data-augmentation for reducing dataset bias in person reidentification, in: *International Conference on Advanced Video and Signal-Based Surveillance*, IEEE (2015), pp. 1–6

[Mes99] MESSER, Kieron; MATAS, Jiri; KITTLER, Josef; LUETTIN, Juergen and MAITRE, Gilbert: XM2VTSDB: The extended M2VTS database, in: *International Conference on Audio and Video-based Biometric Person Authentication*, vol. 964 (1999), pp. 965–966

[Mil10] MILBORROW, S.; MORKEL, J. and NICOLLS, F.: The MUCT Landmarked Face Database. *Pattern Recognition Association of South Africa* (2010), http://www.milbo.org/muct

[Mon98] MONTAVON, Grégoire; ORR, Geneviève B. and MÜLLER, Klaus-Robert (Editors): *Neural Networks: Tricks of the Trade*, vol. 7700 of *LNCS*, Springer, second edition edn. (1998)

[Mud16] MUDUNURI, Sivaram Prasad and BISWAS, Soma: Low Resolution Face Recognition Across Variations in Pose and Illumination. *IEEE Transactions on Pattern Analysis and Machine Intelligence* (2016), vol. 38(5): pp. 1034–1040

[Mud17] MUDUNURI, Sivaram Prasad and BISWAS, Soma: Dictionary Alignment for Low-Resolution and Heterogeneous Face Recognition, in: *Winter Conference on Applications of Computer Vision*, IEEE (2017)

[Nas14] NASROLLAHI, Kamal and MOESLUND, Thomas B: Super-resolution: a comprehensive survey. *Machine vision and applications* (2014), vol. 25(6): pp. 1423–1468

[Nec16] NECH, Aaron and KEMELMACHER-SHLIZERMAN, Ira: Megaface 2: 672,057 Identities for Face Recognition (2016)

[Ng14] NG, Hong-Wei and WINKLER, Stefan: A data-driven approach to cleaning large face datasets, in: *International Conference on Image Processing*, IEEE (2014), pp. 343–347

[Oja02] OJALA, Timo; PIETIKAINEN, Matti and MAENPAA, Topi: Multiresolution gray-scale and rotation invariant texture classification with local binary patterns. *IEEE Transactions on Pattern Analysis and Machine Intelligence* (2002), vol. 24(7): pp. 971–987

[Oja08] OJANSIVU, Ville and HEIKKILÄ, Janne: Blur Insensitive Texture Classification Using Local Phase Quantization, in: *Image and Signal Processing*, Springer (2008), pp. 236–243

[Ort13] ORTIZ, Enrique G; WRIGHT, Alan and SHAH, Mubarak: Face recognition in movie trailers via mean sequence sparse representation-based classification, in: *Conference on Computer Vision and Pattern Recognition*, IEEE (2013)

[Osc14] OSCÓS, Gabriel Castañeda; KHOSHGOFTAAR, Taghi M and WALD, Randall: Rotation invariant face recognition survey, in: *International Conference on Information Reuse and Integration*, IEEE (2014), pp. 835–840

[Ouy16] OUYANG, Shuxin; HOSPEDALES, Timothy; SONG, Yi-Zhe; LI, Xueming; LOY, Chen Change and WANG, Xiaogang: A survey on heterogeneous face recognition: Sketch, infra-red, 3D and low-resolution. *Image and Vision Computing* (2016), vol. 56

[Par14] PARKHI, Omkar M; SIMONYAN, Karen; VEDALDI, Andrea and ZISSERMAN, Andrew: A Compact and Discriminative Face Track Descriptor, in: *Conference on Computer Vision and Pattern Recognition*, IEEE (2014)

[Par15] PARKHI, Omkar M; VEDALDI, Andrea and ZISSERMAN, Andrew: Deep face recognition. *British Machine Vision Conference* (2015), vol. 1(3): p. 6

[Phi00] PHILLIPS, P Jonathon; MOON, Hyeonjoon; RIZVI, Syed A and RAUSS, Patrick J: The FERET evaluation methodology for face-recognition algorithms. *IEEE Transactions on Pattern Analysis and Machine Intelligence* (2000), vol. 22(10): pp. 1090–1104

[Phi03] PHILLIPS, P Jonathon; GROTHER, Patrick; MICHEALS, Ross; BLACKBURN, Duane M; TABASSI, Elham and BONE, Mike: Face recognition vendor test 2002, in: *International Workshop on Analysis and Modeling of Faces and Gestures*, IEEE (2003), p. 44

[Phi05] PHILLIPS, P Jonathon; FLYNN, Patrick J; SCRUGGS, Todd; BOWYER, Kevin W; CHANG, Jin; HOFFMAN, Kevin; MARQUES, Joe; MIN, Jaesik and WOREK, William: Overview of the face recognition grand challenge, in: *Conference on Computer Vision and Pattern Recognition*, vol. 1, IEEE (2005), pp. 947–954

[Phi07a] PHILBIN, James; CHUM, Ondrej; ISARD, Michael; SIVIC, Josef and ZISSERMAN, Andrew: Object retrieval with large vocabularies and fast spatial matching, in: *Conference on Computer Vision and Pattern Recognition*, IEEE (2007), pp. 1–8

[Phi07b] PHILLIPS, P Jonathon; SCRUGGS, W Todd; O'TOOLE, Alice J; FLYNN, Patrick J; BOWYER, Kevin W; SCHOTT, Cathy L and SHARPE, Matthew: FRVT 2006 and ICE 2006 large-scale results. *National Institute of Standards and Technology, NISTIR* (2007), vol. 7408(1)

[Pol02] POLLARD, D.: *A User's Guide to Measure Theoretic Probability*, Cambridge Series in Statistical and Probabilistic Mathematics, Cambridge University Press (2002)

[Qu15] QU, Chengchao; GAO, Hua; MONARI, Eduardo; BEYERER, Jürgen and THIRAN, Jean-Philippe: Towards Robust Cascaded Regression for Face Alignment in the Wild, in: *Conference on Computer Vision and Pattern Recognition Workshops*, IEEE (2015)

[Raj14] RAJAGOPALAN, A.N. and CHELLAPPA, R.: *Motion Deblurring: Algorithms and Systems*, Cambridge University Press (2014)

[Ran16] RANJAN, Rajeev; SANKARANARAYANAN, Swami; CASTILLO, Carlos D and CHELLAPPA, Rama: An All-In-One Convolutional Neural Network for Face Analysis. *arXiv preprint arXiv:1611.00851* (2016)

[Rei13] REID, Daniel; SAMANGOOEI, Sina; CHEN, Cunjian; NIXON, Mark and ROSS, Arun: Soft biometrics for surveillance: an overview. *Machine learning: Theory and Applications. Elsevier* (2013): pp. 327–352

[Ros58] ROSENBLATT, Frank: The perceptron: A probabilistic model for information storage and organization in the brain. *Psychological review* (1958), vol. 65(6): p. 386

[Sam94] SAMARIA, Ferdinando S and HARTER, Andy C: Parameterisation of a stochastic model for human face identification, in: *IEEE Workshop on Applications of Computer Vision*, IEEE (1994), pp. 138–142

[San09] SANDERSON, C. and LOVELL, B.: Multi-region probabilistic histograms for robust and scalable identity inference. *Advances in Biometrics* (2009): pp. 199–208

[Sch14] SCHUMANN, Arne and MONARI, Eduardo: A Soft-Biometrics Dataset for Person Tracking and Re-Identification, in: *International Conference on Advanced Video and Signal-Based Surveillance*, IEEE (2014)

[Sch15a] SCHMIDHUBER, Jürgen: Deep learning in neural networks: An overview. *Neural Networks* (2015), vol. 61: pp. 85–117

[Sch15b] SCHROFF, Florian; KALENICHENKO, Dmitry and PHILBIN, James: FaceNet: A Unified Embedding for Face Recognition and Clustering, in: *Conference on Computer Vision and Pattern Recognition*, IEEE (2015), pp. 815–823

[Sha08] SHAN, Qi; JIA, Jiaya and AGARWALA, Aseem: High-quality motion deblurring from a single image, in: *ACM Transactions on Graphics*, vol. 27, ACM (2008), p. 73

[Sha10] SHAN, Caifeng: Face recognition and retrieval in video, in: *Video Search and Mining*, Springer (2010), pp. 235–260

[Sha11] SHAKHNAROVICH, G. and MOGHADDAM, B.: Face recognition in subspaces. *Handbook of Face Recognition* (2011): pp. 19–49

[She14] SHEKHAR, Sumit; PATEL, Vishal M and CHELLAPPA, Rama: Synthesis-based robust low resolution face recognition. *IEEE Transactions on Image Processing* (2014), vol. 1

[Sim02] SIM, T.; BAKER, S. and BSAT, M.: The CMU pose, illumination, and expression (PIE) database, in: *International Conference on Automatic Face and Gesture Recognition*, IEEE (2002), pp. 46–51

[Sim13] SIMONYAN, Karen; PARKHI, Omkar M; VEDALDI, Andrea and ZISSERMAN, Andrew: Fisher vector faces in the wild, in: *British Machine Vision Conference*, vol. 1 (2013), p. 7

[Sim15] SIMONYAN, Karen and ZISSERMAN, Andrew: Very deep convolutional networks for large-scale image recognition, in: *International Conference on Learning Representations* (2015)

[Sin06] SINHA, Pawan; BALAS, Benjamin; OSTROVSKY, Yuri and RUSSELL, Richard: Face recognition by humans: Nineteen results all computer vision researchers should know about. *Proceedings of the IEEE* (2006), vol. 94(11): pp. 1948–1962

[Siv03] SIVIC, Josef and ZISSERMAN, Andrew: Video Google: A text retrieval approach to object matching in videos, in: *International Conference on Computer Vision*, IEEE (2003), pp. 1470–1477

[Sme14] SMEULDERS, Arnold WM; CHU, Dung M; CUCCHIARA, Rita; CALDERARA, Simone; DEHGHAN, Afshin and SHAH, Mubarak: Visual tracking: An experimental survey. *IEEE Transactions on Pattern Analysis and Machine Intelligence* (2014), vol. 36(7): pp. 1442–1468

[Smi11] SMITH, Brandon M; ZHU, Shengqi and ZHANG, Li: Face image retrieval by shape manipulation, in: *Conference on Computer Vision and Pattern Recognition*, IEEE (2011)

[Smu07] SMUCKER, Mark D; ALLAN, James and CARTERETTE, Ben: A comparison of statistical significance tests for information retrieval evaluation, in: *Information and Knowledge Management* (2007)

[Spa08] SPACEK, Libor: Essex Face Recognition Data (2008), URL http://cswww.essex.ac.uk/mv/allfaces/index.html

[Sri15] SRIVASTAVA, Rupesh K; GREFF, Klaus and SCHMIDHUBER, Jürgen: Training very deep networks, in: *Advances in Neural Information Processing Systems* (2015), pp. 2368–2376

[Sta07] STALLKAMP, Johannes; EKENEL, Hazim K and STIEFELHAGEN, Rainer: Video-based face recognition on real-world data, in: *International Conference on Computer Vision*, IEEE (2007), pp. 1–8

[Sun15] SUN, Yi; WANG, Xiaogang and TANG, Xiaoou: Deeply learned face representations are sparse, selective, and robust, in: *Conference on Computer Vision and Pattern Recognition*, IEEE (2015), pp. 2892–2900

[Sze15a] SZEGEDY, Christian; LIU, Wei; JIA, Yangqing; SERMANET, Pierre; REED, Scott; ANGUELOV, Dragomir; ERHAN, Dumitru; VANHOUCKE, Vincent and RABINOVICH, Andrew: Going deeper with convolutions, in: *Conference on Computer Vision and Pattern Recognition*, IEEE (2015), pp. 1–9

[Sze15b] SZEGEDY, Christian; VANHOUCKE, Vincent; IOFFE, Sergey; SHLENS, Jonathon and WOJNA, Zbigniew: Rethinking the inception architecture for computer vision. *arXiv preprint arXiv:1512.00567* (2015)

[Tai14] TAIGMAN, Yaniv; YANG, Ming; RANZATO, Marc'Aurelio and WOLF, Lior: Deepface: Closing the gap to human-level performance in face verification, in: *Conference on Computer Vision and Pattern Recognition*, IEEE (2014), pp. 1701–1708

[Tan06] TAN, Xiaoyang; CHEN, Songcan; ZHOU, Zhi-Hua and ZHANG, Fuyan: Face recognition from a single image per person: A survey. *Pattern recognition* (2006), vol. 39(9): pp. 1725–1745

[Tap12] TAPASWI, Makarand; BÄUML, M and STIEFELHAGEN, Rainer: "Knock! Knock! Who is it?" probabilistic person identification in TV-series, in: *Conference on Computer Vision and Pattern Recognition*, IEEE (2012), pp. 2658–2665

[Tap14] TAPASWI, Makarand; COREZ, Cemal Cagn; BÄUML, Martin; EKENEL, Hazim Kemal and STIEFELHAGEN, Rainer: Cleaning up after a face tracker: False positive removal, in: *International Conference on Image Processing*, IEEE (2014), pp. 253–257

[Tho10] THOMAZ, Carlos Eduardo and GIRALDI, Gilson Antonio: A new ranking method for principal components analysis and its application to face image analysis. *Image and Vision Computing* (2010), vol. 28(6): pp. 902–913

[Tis09] TISTARELLI, M.; LI, S.Z. and CHELLAPPA, R.: *Handbook of Remote Biometrics: for Surveillance and Security*, Advances in Computer Vision and Pattern Recognition, Springer London (2009)

[Tur91] TURK, M. and PENTLAND, A.: Eigenfaces for Recognition. *Journal of Cognitive Neuroscience* (1991), vol. 3(1): pp. 71–86

[Ull92] ULLMAN, Shimon: Weizmann Face Image Database (1992), URL http://www.wisdom.weizmann.ac.il/~vision/databases.html

[Vai94] VAILLANT, Régis; MONROCQ, Christophe and LE CUN, Yann: Original approach for the localisation of objects in images. *IEEE Proceedings-Vision, Image and Signal Processing* (1994), vol. 141(4): pp. 245–250

[Ved08] VEDALDI, A. and FULKERSON, B.: VLFeat: An Open and Portable Library of Computer Vision Algorithms, http://www.vlfeat.org/ (2008)

[Vio04] VIOLA, Paul and JONES, Michael J: Robust real-time face detection. *International Journal of Computer Vision* (2004), vol. 57(2): pp. 137–154

[Wan05] WANG, Xiaogang and TANG, Xiaoou: Hallucinating face by eigentransformation. *Systems, Man, and Cybernetics, Part C: Applications and Reviews* (2005), vol. 35(3): pp. 425–434

[Wan08] WANG, R.; SHAN, S.; CHEN, X. and GAO, W.: Manifold-manifold distance with application to face recognition based on image set, in: *Conference on Computer Vision and Pattern Recognition*, IEEE (2008), pp. 1–8

[Wan14a] WANG, Nannan; TAO, Dacheng; GAO, Xinbo; LI, Xuelong and LI, Jie: A comprehensive survey to face hallucination. *International Journal of Computer Vision* (2014), vol. 106(1): pp. 9–30

[Wan14b] WANG, Zhifei; MIAO, Zhenjiang; WU, Q. M. Jonathan; WAN, Yanli and TANG, Zhen: Low-resolution face recognition: a review. *The Visual Computer* (2014), vol. 30(4): pp. 359–386

[Wan15] WANG, Wen; WANG, Ruiping; HUANG, Zhiwu; SHAN, Shiguang and CHEN, Xilin: Discriminant analysis on Riemannian manifold of Gaussian distributions for face recognition with image sets, in:

Conference on Computer Vision and Pattern Recognition, IEEE (2015), pp. 2048–2057

[Wan16] WANG, Zhangyang; CHANG, Shiyu; YANG, Yingzhen; LIU, Ding and HUANG, Thomas S: Studying very low resolution recognition using deep networks. *arXiv preprint arXiv:1601.04153* (2016)

[Wec12] WECHSLER, Harry; PHILLIPS, Jonathon P; BRUCE, Vicki; SOULIE, Francoise Fogelman and HUANG, Thomas S: *Face recognition: From theory to applications,* vol. 163, Springer Science & Business Media (2012)

[Wen16] WEN, Yandong; ZHANG, Kaipeng; LI, Zhifeng and QIAO, Yu: A Discriminative Feature Learning Approach for Deep Face Recognition, in: *European Conference on Computer Vision,* Springer (2016), pp. 499–515

[Wib13] WIBOWO, Moh Edi; TJONDRONEGORO, Dian; ZHANG, Ligang and HIMAWAN, Ivan: Heteroscedastic probabilistic linear discriminant analysis for manifold learning in video-based face recognition, in: *Workshop on Applications of Computer Vision* (2013), pp. 46–52

[Wol08] WOLF, Lior; HASSNER, Tal and TAIGMAN, Yaniv: Descriptor based methods in the wild, in: *ECCV Workshop on Faces in Real-Life Images: Detection, Alignment, and Recognition* (2008)

[Wol11] WOLF, L.; HASSNER, T. and MAOZ, I.: Face recognition in unconstrained videos with matched background similarity, in: *Conference on Computer Vision and Pattern Recognition,* IEEE (2011)

[Wol13] WOLF, Lior and LEVY, Noga: The svm-minus similarity score for video face recognition, in: *Conference on Computer Vision and Pattern Recognition,* IEEE (2013)

[Won11] WONG, Yongkang; CHEN, Shaokang; MAU, Sandra; SANDERSON, Conrad and LOVELL, Brian C.: Patch-based Probabilistic Image Quality Assessment for Face Selection and Improved Video-based Face Recognition, in: *Conference on Computer Vision and Pattern Recognition Workshops,* IEEE (2011), pp. 81–88

[Wu11] WU, Zhong; KE, Qifa; SUN, Jian and SHUM, Heung-Yeung: Scalable face image retrieval with identity-based quantization and multireference reranking. *IEEE Transactions on Pattern Analysis and Machine Intelligence* (2011), vol. 33(10): pp. 1991–2001

[Wu16] WU, Junyu; DING, Shengyong; XU, Wei and CHAO, Hongyang: Deep Joint Face Hallucination and Recognition. *arXiv preprint arXiv:1611.08091* (2016)

[Xie06] XIE, Xudong and LAM, Kin-Man: Gabor-based kernel PCA with doubly nonlinear mapping for face recognition with a single face image. *IEEE Transactions on Image Processing* (2006), vol. 15(9): pp. 2481–2492

[Yam98] YAMAGUCHI, O.; FUKUI, K. and MAEDA, K.: Face Recognition Using Temporal Image Sequence, in: *International Conference on Automatic Face and Gesture Recognition*, IEEE (1998)

[Yan02] YANG, M.H.: Face recognition using extended isomap, in: *International Conference on Image Processing*, vol. 2, IEEE (2002), pp. II–117

[Yan04b] YANG, Peng; SHAN, Shiguang; GAO, Wen; LI, Stan Z and ZHANG, Dong: Face recognition using ada-boosted gabor features, in: *International Conference on Automatic Face and Gesture Recognition*, IEEE (2004), pp. 356–361

[Yi14] YI, Dong; LEI, Zhen; LIAO, Shengcai and LI, Stan Z: Learning face representation from scratch. *arXiv preprint arXiv:1411.7923* (2014)

[Zei14] ZEILER, Matthew D and FERGUS, Rob: Visualizing and understanding convolutional networks, in: *European Conference on Computer Vision*, Springer (2014), pp. 818–833

[Zha03b] ZHAO, Wenyi; CHELLAPPA, Rama; PHILLIPS, P Jonathon and ROSENFELD, Azriel: Face recognition: A literature survey. *ACM Computing Surveys* (2003), vol. 35(4): pp. 399–458

[Zha04b] ZHANG, Lei; LI, Stan Z; QU, Zhi Yi and HUANG, Xiangsheng: Boosting Local Feature Based Classifiers For Face Recognition, in: *Conference on Computer Vision and Pattern Recognition Workshops*, IEEE (2004), pp. 87–87

[Zha05] ZHANG, Guangcheng; HUANG, Xiangsheng; LI, Stan Z; WANG, Yangsheng and WU, Xihong: Boosting Local Binary Pattern (LBP)-based Face Recognition, in: *Advances in Biometric Person Authentication*, Springer (2005), pp. 179–186

[Zha08a] ZHAO, M.; YAGNIK, J.; ADAM, H. and BAU, D.: Large Scale Learning and Recognition Of Faces in Web Videos, in: *International Conference on Automatic Face and Gesture Recognition*, IEEE (2008), pp. 1–7

[Zha09] ZHANG, X. and GAO, Y.: Face recognition across pose: A review. *Pattern Recognition* (2009), vol. 42(11): pp. 2876–2896

[Zha11] ZHAO, W. and CHELLAPPA, R.: *Face Processing: Advanced Modeling and Methods*, Elsevier Science (2011)

[Zha12a] ZHANG, Xiao; ZHANG, Lei; WANG, Xin-Jing and SHUM, Heung-Yeung: Finding celebrities in billions of web images. *IEEE Transactions on Multimedia* (2012), vol. 14(4): pp. 995–1007

[Zhe16] ZHENG, Lilei: *Triangular Similarity Metric Learning: a Siamese Architecture Approach*, Ph.D. thesis, Université de Lyon (2016)

[Zho06] ZHOU, Shaohua Kevin and CHELLAPPA, Rama: From sample similarity to ensemble similarity: Probabilistic distance measures in reproducing kernel hilbert space. *IEEE Transactions on Pattern Analysis and Machine Intelligence* (2006), vol. 28(6): pp. 917–929

[Zho14] ZHOU, Hailing; MIAN, Ajmal; WEI, Lei; CREIGHTON, Doug; HOSSNY, Mo and NAHAVANDI, Saeid: Recent advances on single-modal and multimodal face recognition: A survey. *IEEE Transactions on Human-Machine Systems* (2014), vol. 44(6): pp. 701–716

[Zou07a] ZOU, Jie; JI, Qiang and NAGY, George: A Comparative Study of Local Matching Approach for Face Recognition. *IEEE Transactions on Image Processing* (2007), vol. 16(10): pp. 2617–2628

[Zou07b] ZOU, Xuan; KITTLER, Josef and MESSER, Kieron: Illumination invariant face recognition: A survey, in: *International Conference on Biometrics: Theory, Applications and Systems*, IEEE (2007), pp. 1–8

Publications

[Gün17] GÜNTHER, Manuel; HU, Peiyun; HERRMANN, Christian; CHAN, Chi Ho; JIANG, Min; YANG, Shufan; DHAMIJA, Akshay Raj; RAMANAN, Deva; BEYERER, Jürgen; KITTLER, Josef; JAZAERY, M.; NOUYED, M.I.; GUO, G.; STANKIEWICZ, C. and BOULT, T.E.: Unconstrained Face Detection and Open-Set Face Recognition Challenge, in: *International Joint Conference on Biometrics* (2017)

[Her11] HERRMANN, Christian; MANGER, Daniel and METZLER, Jürgen: Feature-based localization refinement of players in soccer using plausibility maps, in: *Proc. of International Conference on Image Processing, Computer Vision, and Pattern Recognition IPCV*, vol. 2 (2011)

[Her12] HERRMANN, Christian; METZLER, Jürgen and WILLERSINN, Dieter: Semi-Automatic People Counting in Aerial Images of Large Crowds, in: *Proc. SPIE 8542, Electro-Optical Remote Sensing, Photonic Technologies, and Applications VI*, International Society for Optics and Photonics (2012), p. 85420Q

[Her13a] HERRMANN, Christian: Extending a Local Matching Face Recognition Approach to Low-Resolution Video, in: *International Conference on Advanced Video and Signal-Based Surveillance*, IEEE (2013)

[Her13b] HERRMANN, Christian and METZLER, Jürgen: Density Estimation in Aerial Images of Large Crowds for Automatic People Counting, in: *Proc. SPIE 8713, Airborne Intelligence, Surveillance, Reconnaissance (ISR) Systems and Applications X,* International Society for Optics and Photonics (2013), p. 87130V

[Her14a] HERRMANN, Christian and BEYERER, Jürgen: Maximizing Face Recognition Performance for Video Data under Time Constraints by Using a Cascade, in: *International Conference on Advanced Video and Signal-Based Surveillance,* IEEE (2014), pp. 181–186

[Her14b] HERRMANN, Christian and BEYERER, Jürgen: Pyramid Mean Representation of Image Sequences for Fast Face Retrieval in Unconstrained Video Data, in: *International Symposium on Visual Computing,* Springer (2014), pp. 304–314

[Her15a] HERRMANN, Christian and BEYERER, Jürgen: Face Retrieval on Large-Scale Video Data, in: *Canadian Conference on Computer and Robot Vision,* IEEE (2015), pp. 192–199

[Her15b] HERRMANN, Christian and BEYERER, Jürgen: Fast Face Recognition by Using an Inverted Index, in: *Proc. SPIE 9405, Image Processing: Machine Vision Applications VIII,* International Society for Optics and Photonics (2015), p. 940507

[Her15c] HERRMANN, Christian; METZLER, Jürgen; WILLERSINN, Dieter and BEYERER, Jürgen: Face- and Appearance-Based Person Identification for Forensic Analysis of Surveillance Videos, in: *Future Security* (2015)

[Her15d] HERRMANN, Christian; QU, Chengchao and BEYERER, Jürgen: Low-Resolution Video Face Recognition with Face Normalization and Feature Adaptation, in: *International Conference on Signal and Image Processing Applications,* IEEE (2015)

[Her15e] HERRMANN, Christian; QU, Chengchao; WILLERSINN, Dieter and BEYERER, Jürgen: Impact of Resolution and Image Quality on Video Face Analysis, in: *International Conference on Advanced Video and Signal-Based Surveillance,* IEEE (2015)

[Her16a] HERRMANN, Christian; MÜLLER, Thomas; WILLERSINN, Dieter and BEYERER, Jürgen: Real-Time Person Detection in Low-Resolution Thermal Infrared Imagery with MSER and CNNs, in:

Proc. SPIE 9987, Electro-Optical and Infrared Systems: Technology and Applications, International Society for Optics and Photonics (2016)

[Her16b] HERRMANN, Christian; WILLERSINN, Dieter and BEYERER, Jürgen: Low-Quality Video Face Recognition with Deep Networks and Polygonal Chain Distance, in: *Digital Image Computing: Techniques and Applications,* IEEE (2016)

[Her16c] HERRMANN, Christian; WILLERSINN, Dieter and BEYERER, Jürgen: Low-Resolution Convolutional Neural Networks for Video Face Recognition, in: *International Conference on Advanced Video and Signal-Based Surveillance,* IEEE (2016)

[Her17] HERRMANN, Christian; WILLERSINN, Dieter and BEYERER, Jürgen: Residual vs. Inception vs. Classical Networks for Low-Resolution Face Recognition, in: *Scandinavian Conference on Image Analysis,* Springer (2017), pp. 377–388

[Man16] MANGER, Daniel; HERRMANN, Christian and WILLERSINN, Dieter: Towards Extending Bag-of-Words-Models Using Context Features for an 2D Inverted Index, in: *Digital Image Computing: Techniques and Applications,* IEEE (2016)

[Qu15] QU, Chengchao; HERRMANN, Christian; MONARI, Eduardo; SCHUCHERT, Tobias and BEYERER, Jürgen: 3D vs. 2D: On the Importance of Registration for Hallucinating Faces under Unconstrained Poses, in: *Canadian Conference on Computer and Robot Vision,* IEEE (2015)

[Qu17] QU, Chengchao; HERRMANN, Christian; MONARI, Eduardo; SCHUCHERT, Tobias and BEYERER, Jürgen: Robust 3D Patch-Based Face Hallucination, in: *Winter Conference on Applications of Computer Vision,* IEEE (2017), pp. 1105–1114

Acronyms

AUC Area Under the Curve

CNN Convolutional Neural Network

DCT Discrete Cosine Transform

EER Equal Error Rate

GMM Gaussian Mixture Model

HOG Histogram of Oriented Gradients

HR high-resolution

IJB-A IARPA Janus Benchmark-A

LBP Local Binary Patterns

LDP Local Directional Patterns

LFW Labeled Faces in the Wild

LLE Locally Linear Embedding

LMM Local Mean Method

LqfNet Low-Quality Face Network

LR low-resolution

LrfNet Low-Resolution Face Network

LTP Local Ternary Patterns

MAC Multiply-and-Accumulate

MCT Modified Census Transform

MLP Multilayer Perceptron

MS1M MS-Celeb-1M

MSM Mutual Subspace Method

MSRA MSRA-CFW

NIST National Institute of Standards and Technology

PCA Principal Component Analysis

ReLU Rectified Linear Unit

ROC Receiver Operating Characteristic

SIFT Scale-Invariant Feature Transform

t-SNE t-Distributed Stochastic Neighbor Embedding

TVC TV Collection

VGG Visual Geometry Group

YTF YouTube Faces Database

Table of Symbols

$\wedge$	logical and
$\Leftrightarrow$	logical equivalence / if and only if
$\vee$	logical or
$\sim$	distributed according to

Calligraphic Symbols

$\mathcal{B}$	batch
$\mathcal{C}$	face image descriptor method
$\mathcal{D}$	general notation for a distance
$\mathcal{D}_c$	Cosine distance
$\mathcal{D}_e$	Euclidean distance
$\mathcal{D}_h$	Hellinger distance
$\mathcal{I}$	identity function assigning the person identity to a face sample
$\mathcal{L}$	Laplacian filter
$\mathcal{N}$	normal distribution
$\mathcal{O}$	Big O notation / Bachmann-Landau notation

$\mathcal{Q}$	query object
$\mathcal{S}$	similarity score
$\mathcal{V}$	face image descriptor
$\mathcal{W}$	face sequence descriptor

Greek Symbols

α	significance level
α,β,γ	rotation angles
δ	LBP radius sampling density
η	decision boundary
κ	number of local centers
μ	cluster center
ψ	learning rate
ρ	prediction value
θ	verification threshold
$\boldsymbol{\varphi}$	bag-of-words vector
$\boldsymbol{\xi}$	global coordinates of a measurement $(X,Y,Z)^T$
$\boldsymbol{\omega}$	perceptron weight vector

Roman Symbols

acc	verification accuracy
ap	average precision
std	standard deviation
FN	false negatives
FNR	false negative rate
FP	false positives

FPR	false positive rate
Pr	precision
Re	recall
TN	true negatives
TP	true positives
TPR	true positive rate
a	upper bound of intra-class distance
b	bias
c	number of active domain augmentations
d	descriptor dimension
g	distance of sensor to projection center (intrinsic pinhole camera parameter)
h	region or image height
k	cross-validation folds
$k \times k$	receptive field size
l_w, l_h	number of local regions in width and height
m	number of queries
n	number of elements
o_x, o_y	sensor origin (intrinsic pinhole camera parameters)
p	number of LBP neighborhood points
q	local feature dimension
r	radius
s	image sharpness level
s_x, s_y	pixel scales (intrinsic pinhole camera parameters)
t_q	query duration

u, v	image coordinates
v	number of vertex points
w	region or image width
x, y, z	camera coordinates
y	perceptron output
y_{ij}	indicator variable
B	bins in LBP histogram
C	person identity
F	number of features per sequence
G	meta-parameter for number of filters per convolutional layer
H	meta-parameter for number of neurons per fully connected layer
I	inverted index
I_C	set of all descriptors for identity C
J	diagonal weight matrix for encoding
K	codebook size
L	loss function
N	number of elements
N_b	number of layer blocks
N_c	number of convolutional layers
N_f	number of fully connected layers
N_g	number of layer groups
N_{out}	classes in CNN classifier
O	retrieval object in database
P	pooling region size
Q	retrieval ranking

R	rotation matrix
T	sequence of face image vectors
W	neural network layer weight matrix
X, Y, Z	global coordinates
$\boldsymbol{b}$	bias vector
$\boldsymbol{h}$	local feature vector
$\boldsymbol{m}$	mean vector
$\boldsymbol{t}$	translation vector
$\boldsymbol{u}$	face image vector
$\boldsymbol{v}$	face image descriptor vector
$\boldsymbol{w}$	face sequence descriptor vector
$\boldsymbol{x}$	perceptron input vector
$\boldsymbol{y}$	neural network output

Karlsruher Schriftenreihe zur Anthropomatik (ISSN 1863-6489)

Herausgeber: Prof. Dr.-Ing. habil. Jürgen Beyerer

Band 1 Jürgen Geisler
Leistung des Menschen am Bildschirmarbeitsplatz. 2006
ISBN 3-86644-070-7

Band 2 Elisabeth Peinsipp-Byma
Leistungserhöhung durch Assistenz in interaktiven Systemen zur Szenenanalyse. 2007
ISBN 978-3-86644-149-1

Band 3 Jürgen Geisler, Jürgen Beyerer (Hrsg.)
Mensch-Maschine-Systeme. 2010
ISBN 978-3-86644-457-7

Band 4 Jürgen Beyerer, Marco Huber (Hrsg.)
Proceedings of the 2009 Joint Workshop of Fraunhofer IOSB and Institute for Anthropomatics, Vision and Fusion Laboratory. 2010
ISBN 978-3-86644-469-0

Band 5 Thomas Usländer
Service-oriented design of environmental information systems. 2010
ISBN 978-3-86644-499-7

Band 6 Giulio Milighetti
Multisensorielle diskret-kontinuierliche Überwachung und Regelung humanoider Roboter. 2010
ISBN 978-3-86644-568-0

Band 7 Jürgen Beyerer, Marco Huber (Hrsg.)
Proceedings of the 2010 Joint Workshop of Fraunhofer IOSB and Institute for Anthropomatics, Vision and Fusion Laboratory. 2011
ISBN 978-3-86644-609-0

Band 8 Eduardo Monari
Dynamische Sensorselektion zur auftragsorientierten Objektverfolgung in Kameranetzwerken. 2011
ISBN 978-3-86644-729-5

Die Bände sind unter www.ksp.kit.edu als PDF frei verfügbar oder als Druckausgabe bestellbar.

Band 9 Thomas Bader
Multimodale Interaktion in Multi-Display-Umgebungen. 2011
ISBN 3-86644-760-8

Band 10 Christian Frese
Planung kooperativer Fahrmanöver für kognitive Automobile. 2012
ISBN 978-3-86644-798-1

Band 11 Jürgen Beyerer, Alexey Pak (Hrsg.)
Proceedings of the 2011 Joint Workshop of Fraunhofer IOSB and Institute for Anthropomatics, Vision and Fusion Laboratory. 2012
ISBN 978-3-86644-855-1

Band 12 Miriam Schleipen
Adaptivität und Interoperabilität von Manufacturing Execution Systemen (MES). 2013
ISBN 978-3-86644-955-8

Band 13 Jürgen Beyerer, Alexey Pak (Hrsg.)
Proceedings of the 2012 Joint Workshop of Fraunhofer IOSB and Institute for Anthropomatics, Vision and Fusion Laboratory. 2013
ISBN 978-3-86644-988-6

Band 14 Hauke-Hendrik Vagts
Privatheit und Datenschutz in der intelligenten Überwachung: Ein datenschutzgewährendes System, entworfen nach dem „Privacy by Design" Prinzip. 2013
ISBN 978-3-7315-0041-4

Band 15 Christian Kühnert
Data-driven Methods for Fault Localization in Process Technology. 2013
ISBN 978-3-7315-0098-8

Band 16 Alexander Bauer
Probabilistische Szenenmodelle für die Luftbildauswertung. 2014
ISBN 978-3-7315-0167-1

Band 17 Jürgen Beyerer, Alexey Pak (Hrsg.)
Proceedings of the 2013 Joint Workshop of Fraunhofer IOSB and Institute for Anthropomatics, Vision and Fusion Laboratory. 2014
ISBN 978-3-7315-0212-8

Band 18 Michael Teutsch
Moving Object Detection and Segmentation for Remote Aerial Video Surveillance. 2015
ISBN 978-3-7315-0320-0

Band 19 Marco Huber
Nonlinear Gaussian Filtering: Theory, Algorithms, and Applications. 2015
ISBN 978-3-7315-0338-5

Band 20 Jürgen Beyerer, Alexey Pak (Hrsg.)
Proceedings of the 2014 Joint Workshop of Fraunhofer IOSB and Institute for Anthropomatics, Vision and Fusion Laboratory. 2014
ISBN 978-3-7315-0401-6

Band 21 Todor Dimitrov
Permanente Optimierung dynamischer Probleme der Fertigungssteuerung unter Einbeziehung von Benutzerinteraktionen. 2015
ISBN 978-3-7315-0426-9

Band 22 Benjamin Kühn
Interessengetriebene audiovisuelle Szenenexploration. 2016
ISBN 978-3-7315-0457-3

Band 23 Yvonne Fischer
Wissensbasierte probabilistische Modellierung für die Situationsanalyse am Beispiel der maritimen Überwachung. 2016
ISBN 978-3-7315-0460-3

Band 24 Jürgen Beyerer, Alexey Pak (Hrsg.)
Proceedings of the 2015 Joint Workshop of Fraunhofer IOSB and Institute for Anthropomatics, Vision and Fusion Laboratory. 2016
ISBN 978-3-7315-0519-8

Band 25 Pascal Birnstill
Privacy-Respecting Smart Video Surveillance Based on Usage Control Enforcement. 2016
ISBN 978-3-7315-0538-9

Band 26 Philipp Woock
Umgebungskartenschätzung aus Sidescan-Sonardaten für ein autonomes Unterwasserfahrzeug. 2016
ISBN 978-3-7315-0541-9

Band 27 Janko Petereit
Adaptive State × Time Lattices: A Contribution to Mobile Robot Motion Planning in Unstructured Dynamic Environments. 2017
ISBN 978-3-7315-0580-8

Band 28 Erik Ludwig Krempel
Steigerung der Akzeptanz von intelligenter Videoüberwachung in öffentlichen Räumen. 2017
ISBN 978-3-7315-0598-3

Band 29 Jürgen Moßgraber
Ein Rahmenwerk für die Architektur von Frühwarnsystemen. 2017
ISBN 978-3-7315-0638-6

Band 30 Andrey Belkin
World Modeling for Intelligent Autonomous Systems. 2017
ISBN 978-3-7315-0641-6

Band 31 Chettapong Janya-Anurak
Framework for Analysis and Identification of Nonlinear Distributed Parameter Systems using Bayesian Uncertainty Quantification based on Generalized Polynomial Chaos. 2017
ISBN 978-3-7315-0642-3

Band 32 David Münch
Begriffliche Situationsanalyse aus Videodaten bei unvollständiger und fehlerhafter Information. 2017
ISBN 978-3-7315-0644-7

Band 33 Jürgen Beyerer, Alexey Pak (Eds.)
Proceedings of the 2016 Joint Workshop of Fraunhofer IOSB and Institute for Anthropomatics, Vision and Fusion Laboratory. 2017
ISBN 978-3-7315-0678-2

Band 34 Jürgen Beyerer, Alexey Pak and Miro Taphanel (Eds.)
Proceedings of the 2017 Joint Workshop of Fraunhofer IOSB and Institute for Anthropomatics, Vision and Fusion Laboratory. 2018
ISBN 978-3-7315-0779-6

Band 35 Michael Grinberg
Feature-Based Probabilistic Data Association for Video-Based Multi-Object Tracking. 2018
ISBN 978-3-7315-0781-9

Band 36 Christian Herrmann
Video-to-Video Face Recognition for Low-Quality Surveillance Data. 2018
ISBN 978-3-7315-0799-4

Die Bände sind unter www.ksp.kit.edu als PDF frei verfügbar oder als Druckausgabe bestellbar.